At a time when COVID has pushed examples of what "Doing" looks like. They have personalized the voices of need from around the globe—from homeless orphans to health workers— and, true to their mission, they have opened doors enabling countless others to see possibility in the midst of pain and seize opportunities to help. Their creation—Assist International—is a thriving catalyst that has transformed willing resource into tangible, life-saving change for literally millions of people. As their mission continues to evolve, the Pagett's story calls us to join in and be part of what is possible.

— **Krista (Bauer) St George**
VP Product Management, SI Group;
Formerly Director of Global Programs, GE

The word "leap" connotes the image of two people hand-in-hand jumping from a high cliff—knowing there is water below but not knowing the height of the cliff nor the depth of the water. Bob and Char took a hand-in-hand leap when they founded Assist International. I was privileged to be involved in A.I. since its infancy and continue to be amazed with its global influence over 30 years later. This book is the story of the impact two people can make when they are willing to take a leap and believe. Bob and Char's journey will strengthen your faith, increase your resolve to make a difference in our world, and inspire you to take your own leap.

— **Dr. Michael Comer**
- President of The Hayes Group International,
AI Board Member, co-author of *Start with Humility:
Lessons from America's Quiet CEOs on
How to Build Trust and Inspire Followers*

When Bob Pagett contacted me to ask me to write an endorsement of *Leap of Faith* was a few days from flying to Ethiopia to dedicate a Rotary project to provide an Oxygen Generation Plant serving 15 hospitals that would not have been possible without Bob Pagett. When I brought a young nurse born in Ethiopia to Bob to explain this need and impossible task, Bob's connections, knowledge, and positive encouragement made it a reality. I could not say "no" to Bob and read the manuscript. This page-turner book is full of wonderful stories about Bob and Char and how their ability to connect and inspire others has changed and saved lives around the world. I highly recommend this book. I have traveled with Bob and Char on projects in Djibouti, Laos, China, and Romania and witnessed their amazing leadership skills. They are humble, but larger than life, heroic individuals who deserve to have their story shared. Readers will be inspired to make the world a better place.

— Joe Hamilton
- Rotary District 5170 District Governor 2012-13

I have been fortunate enough to walk alongside Bob where he introduced me to the humanity efforts he has been involved with in Romania and Uganda. It is impossible to calculate the number of lives he positively affected thru his ministry. I have never met a more Godly and humble man than Bob Pagett. I feel truly blessed to call him my friend.

— Jim Sankey - CEO InVue

The path traveled by Bob and Charlene Pagett around the globe to meet the challenges of the world's most vulnerable people would never be possible without their unwavering faith in a loving God who cares deeply for the suffering. The pages of this book tell the remarkable story of two ordinary people who dared to make a difference. This book will inspire you to believe that through the same simple faith, you can make a difference too.

— Sharon M. Fruh, Ph.D., RN, FNP-BC, FAANP,
Professor, Associate Dean for Research, Evaluation, and Development, University of South Alabama, College of Nursing

In order to find [the] right book you want to read, just search for one that encourages you to have a 'Leap of Faith.'

This book has appropriate words and messages behind every sentence which will enrich your faith. The uniqueness of this book lies in the authors who, like Abraham the father of our faith, believe God would do whatever he said. Bob and Charlene too, in faith, believe nothing is impossible and difficult with God.

They encourage all of us to trust in God and keep insisting on doing what God calls us to do in spreading his kingdom. In life we must be ever ready to leave with this kind of faith which makes us embrace a path least explored because we trust in God.

Leap of Faith is a must-read book because our journey on earth fills us with lots of doubts which can deviate our attention from following the path that can make us live with hope for the future.

— Sr. Rosemary Nyirumbe
- Director of St. Monica and Sewing Projects
In partnership with Assist International founded by Bob and Charlene

LEAP
of
FAITH

THE STORY OF
**Bob and
Charlene Pagett,**
FOUNDERS OF
Assist International

BY
WILLIAM
AND NANCIE CARMICHAEL

Deep*River*
B O O K S

All Scripture quotations, unless otherwise noted, are taken from the Holy Bible, New International Version®, NIV® Copyright ©1973, 1978, 1984, 2011 by Biblica, Inc.® Used by permission. All rights reserved worldwide.

Scripture quotations marked KJV are taken from the King James Version. Public domain.

Scripture quotations marked MSG are taken from *THE MESSAGE*, copyright © 1993, 2002, 2018 by Eugene H. Peterson. Used by permission of NavPress. All rights reserved. Represented by Tyndale House Publishers, Inc.

Scripture quotations marked TLB are taken from The Living Bible, copyright © 1971 by Tyndale House Foundation. Used by permission of Tyndale House Publishers Inc., Carol Stream, Illinois 60188. All rights reserved.

Scripture quotations marked NKJV are taken from the New King James Version®. Copyright © 1982 by Thomas Nelson. Used by permission. All rights reserved.

Scripture quotations marked NLT are taken from the *Holy Bible*, New Living Translation, copyright © 1996, 2004, 2015 by Tyndale House Foundation. Used by permission of Tyndale House Publishers, Inc., Carol Stream, Illinois 60188. All rights reserved.

Scripture quotations marked NASB are taken from the New American Standard Bible®, Copyright © 1960, 1971, 1977, 1995, 2020 by The Lockman Foundation. All rights reserved.

Cover design by Jason Enterline

ISBN—13: 9781632695840
Library of Congress Control Number: 2022901141

Printed in the USA
2022—First Edition
31 30 29 28 27 26 25 24 23 22   10 9 8 7 6 5 4 3 2 1

DEDICATION

To the memory of Pamela Renee Pagett,
our third daughter, who was taken from us too soon,
but who taught us what love can be.

She Was an Angel

She was an angel, Pamela Renee. . .
even her name sounds angelic.
Today, we grieve her loss, but she has given
us far more than grief or sorrow.
She didn't visit long enough to learn to speak—
but in her unspoken words is a beautiful message. . . .
Her message is one of love, for in loving her she has increased our
capacity to love—not just her,
but all those who beckon for love. . . .
Her message is one of joy, in remembering
the blessed hope of making heaven our home
where sorrow is unknown, and we can reunite with her. . . .
Her message is one of peace, for in our sorrow,
the Holy Spirit gives us the
"Peace which passes understanding.". . .
Her message is one of longsuffering, for in grieving her loss
we learn new capacities to understand the loss of others. . . .
Finally, her message is one of trust, in HIM. . .
that He knows best,
however confused and dark today may seem. . .
Granted, she was just an infant—but in her brief visit to us,
she has illumined the very FRUIT OF HIS SPIRIT.
Her visit is over, but her message lives on.
For you see. . . she was an angel.[1]

TABLE OF CONTENTS

A NOTE FROM BOB AND CHARLENE

These are stories based on our memories, which may be imperfect. We are the first to say we are ten years too late in relaying these stories. There may be parts that are oversimplified or out of sequence. There will be parts that others may remember differently. Read this book the way you would receive grandparents reminiscing around a campfire.

FOREWORD

From toasted cheese sandwiches and soup at 2 a.m. on New Year's Day 1957 in a Colorado town to impacting the nations of the world in 2022 is indeed a leap. And faith is clearly the engine.

As I read Bob and Char Pagett's story, I kept hearing the words of one of their friends—a man who has served at the highest level of leadership in our land, who said this: *"Leaders are people who select noble objectives and pursue them with such intensity and sacrifice that they carry other people with them."*

In their passionate, persistent, and winsome ways Bob and Char are those leaders. I have known them for decades—as a parishioner at their church in Santa Cruz, colleague in college leadership, and traveler to Romania with them to meet with government leaders, and—most of all—as a friend.

They bring hope to the world on the ground. How real they are. They challenge you, weep with you, and laugh with you. And the atmosphere never changes.

It shows in the ways they have stepped out—again and again—by themselves, but never ended up by themselves. When you read their story, you meet a ton of their friends. I love it.

They have never been afraid to trust God nor to invite others to trust God with them in their mission to share light and life through Jesus to the nations. How inspiring that is.

If you desire a fresh breath of the Spirit to sweep your soul, read this book!

—Dick Foth

CHAPTER ONE

TWO EXTRAORDINARY PEOPLE

*The life of faith is not a life of mounting up with
wings, but a life of walking and not fainting. It is. . .
faith that has been tried and proved and stood the test.*

—**Oswald Chambers**, *My Utmost for His Highest*[2]

This is a story about two extraordinary people. Well, sort of.
In most ways they are ordinary like all of us. But what sets
them apart is that when most people in their fifties are thinking
of slowing down, Bob and Char Pagett took a leap of faith into
the unknown and consequently, their lives have helped change
the world. Their story and the story of the founding of Assist
International, the organization they founded in 1990, continues
to change the world in various and wonderful ways.

When you think of world-renowned nonprofit humanitarian
organizations, Assist International may be one you haven't heard
about. Part of that is because the founders have never wanted nor

sought recognition for what they started thirty years ago. Their goal has always been to network with others and recognize them for the good they do for vulnerable people in the world. Another reason for being under the radar is because they, along with their entire staff, see themselves as helpers called to serve others. And they simply haven't had the desire to seek their own recognition. They've been too busy assisting others!

Assist International operates primarily out of a 30,000-square-foot warehouse-office complex in Ripon, a small town in California along old Highway 99, known more for its almond orchards, dairy farms, and truck stops than it is for this nonprofit organization.

Bob and Char are the first to insist that nothing they have done has been on their own—that in establishing Assist International, their story and the story of Assist International is filled with "God-stories." And while Assist International freely works with people and cultures of all faiths, without discrimination, it has been founded on the deep personal Christian faith of Bob and Char Pagett.

This is their story.

You will find in this account Bob and Char's personal faith story and the core of their lives that has driven them to do what they have done. You will discover surprising principles you won't find on the Assist International website, and you will see how Assist International has come to exist.

Bob and Char's son-in-law Ralph Sudfeld, president of Assist International, said, "I am blessed to have Bob and Char in my life. They live their lives as examples of what faith in action looks like. Throughout their lives, they've displayed an exceptional heart for people. They overflow with love and compassion. And when this compassion collided with a leap of faith, Assist International was born.

"The story of Bob and Char's founding of Assist International is a story of faith, optimism, and the belief that every person in the world is valuable. It's a story of perseverance, of overcoming challenges and obstacles, all in the pursuit of the greater good. It's a story of togetherness, connecting people from different backgrounds and different countries to join in the effort to save lives and impact communities."

Bob and Char have always worked with all people, of all faiths or no faith at all, and their life mission is to help the most vulnerable people in the world, especially children, wherever they are found, without regard to race, religion, or political system. We've seen clearly that the foundational motive for the work they started to help others was born out of their love for God and what their personal faith taught them about the priority to care for widows, orphans, and those hungry and in need.

Mitch Albom, author of *Tuesdays with Morrie*, observed, "So many people walk around with a meaningless life. They seem half-asleep, even when they're busy doing things they think are important. This is because they're chasing the wrong things. The way you get meaning to your life is to devote yourself to loving others. . . devote yourself to creating something that gives you purpose and meaning."[3]

Bob and Char lead lives of profound meaning and joy. It is the kind of life we all yearn to live—lives that make a difference. You might think that they would be serious, duty-bound souls, driven and exhausted from trying to meet so many huge needs. But we see quite the opposite. They laugh a lot. They have fun. Char loves to ride roller coasters. Bob is intrigued with history and could write a suspense novel if only he had time. But most of all, their hearts are challenged by seeing vulnerable people in need, and with a sense of joy and adventure, engaging their faith to see those needs met.

Leaps of faith begin with steps of faith. Sometimes exceedingly small steps. But small, persistent steps in the right direction can ultimately have a big impact. As Robert Frost wrote, "Way leads on to way." Big things happen when people who want to make a difference are willing to see a need and are committed to do something about it. And passion for a cause can be contagious. So, how gratifying it is to empower others along the way, which exponentially accomplishes more—reaches more.

And so it has been for Assist International under the leadership of Bob and Char Pagett. In these thirty years since it began, astounding things have happened. Here are a few of the things that have been accomplished (and are being accomplished):

- *More than six hundred projects in sixty countries.* Networking with more than five hundred partners—including major corporations, service organizations, universities, other NGOs, and government agencies as well as people of all faiths and individual donors—have impacted thousands of lives.

- *Vulnerable children have new homes.* Working with overseas organizations such as Caminul Felix Villages in Oradea, Romania and Felix Family Village in Surat Thani, Thailand; Jesus, Hope of Romania (JHOR) and Onemimus House in Timisorara, Romania; Sister Rosemary Nyriumbe's Sewing Hope Children's Village (Orphan Village) in Uganda; AIDS Orphan Education Trust (AOET) in Jinja, Uganda; and Otino-Waa Village in Lira, Uganda, Assist International has built sixty-nine homes, each one housing from eight to eighteen children who are loved and cared for by house parents who care for them as their own.

In Assist International's thirty years of service, these homes have given thousands of vulnerable children new hope and opportunity. Many of these children, now raised, have worked in business, some starting their own businesses and some becoming doctors, lawyers, various health professionals, teachers, pastors, and many other productive professionals, as well as loving parents to their own children. And these homes continue to help parent vulnerable children. In the first village where Assist International built orphan homes in Romania, one of the young men raised there has now grown, and together with his wife have become house parents themselves in an orphan village home two doors down from the one he was raised in. His incredible story will be told.

- *Global health needs addressed.* Assist International has been a key partner to projects that develop medical infrastructure and clinical services, impacting more than eleven million people in thirty-three health facilities. Their work has also helped to train 480 biomedical engineers and trained hundreds of nurses and other health workers in more than three hundred health facilities in thirty-six countries. They have also accomplished multiple safe water projects for health facilities across seven countries.

- *Desperately needed supplies provided.* Hundreds of shipping containers have gone to all parts of the world where the most vulnerable live. Food, medicine, clothing, bedding, furnishings, and all types of new medical equipment such as heart monitors, central stations, anesthesia machines, pulse oximeters, CT scanners, Xray machines, baby warmers, incubators, defibrillators, operating tables,

surgical lights, birthing tables, electrocardiograms, ventila-
tors, power generators and transformers, water treatment
plants, and clean surgical hospital building additions. They
have also supplied hundreds of bicycle-powered irrigation
systems to farmers in Africa.

These statistics mean the difference between life and death to
real people. Statistics only reflect part of what has been accomplished working in partnership with local ministries of health,
along with key partnerships as noted above. The impact is impossible to measure on a human scale.

But as we said, steps of faith usually start small, starting where
we are and with what we have. Bob and Char are amazed as they
remember that it all started in a spare bedroom of their home with
a telephone, a fax machine, and a strong faith in God and humanity. It all started with seeing a need that was bigger than they
were—but with a leap of faith in a God who they knew would
never fail them.

As you read their story, you will see the basic principles that
have guided Bob and Charlene Pagett in their "leap of faith," as
well as some of their most inspiring and incredible experiences.
Hopefully, you too will be inspired to take steps of faith where you
are to make a difference in your world.

Bob and Charlene's story encompasses so many other stories—
stories of other people, and their wanting to make a difference too.
It would be impossible to include in this book all the stories we
received about Assist International and its projects around the world
in more than thirty years of service. It would also be impossible to
name and give credit to all the individuals who have contributed
to Assist International in so many ways—giving of their resources,
time, expertise, prayers, and compassion for others.

Some key contacts in various countries and major financial contributors who have given and continue to give sacrificially remain anonymous. It would be unwise to name them, as some wish to remain anonymous for personal or corporate reasons. Hence, we have omitted names of organizations, individuals, and in some cases even countries where events took place. If you are one of these who remain anonymous, you know who you are, and Bob and Char are profoundly grateful for you and your personal sacrifice and contribution to the work of Assist International. They recognize that all that has been accomplished in the world through Assist International is because the partnership with all of you: the donors, organizations, foundations, board members, staff, and volunteers across the spectrum who have made this incredible journey possible.

The stories we share illustrate some basic principles that have allowed Bob and Char's vision to succeed beyond anyone's dreams and to assist others who may be on the edge of their vision for the future.

In 1990, I (Bill) was asked to be the vice president of the board of directors of Assist International Inc., a new 501(c)3 not-for-profit entity. I held that position for twenty-five of Assist International's thirty years of existence, which has given me intimate and up-front insights into its development. My wife Nancie and I have also been on overseas trips with Assist International and have seen firsthand many of the accomplishments that have taken place. We have watched the staff develop and the unavoidable trials and challenges associated with their incredible accomplishments.

Another reason we know their story well is that we have been witnesses to it for most of our lives. Char is my (Bill's) sister, and Bob (who has had to put up with me since I was age twelve is in every way except biological), my big brother. There is no one I respect and admire more than my big brother Bob!

The more we know their story, the more amazed and grateful we are to see the ripple effect of their faith, and of their commitment to serve and empower others to make a difference in the world. It is heartwarming to see so many others who have joined the cause and have walked with Bob and Char through the years. It is also wonderful to see how their children and grandchildren have caught the vision, as they are now taking the reins to continue the story of making a difference and empowering other people and organizations along the way who are also making a difference for the vulnerable in the world.

Since we come from a publishing and writing background, we were asked to write their story. It is an honor and privilege to tell the story of Bob and Char Pagett, and their contagious story of faith.

Bill and Nancie Carmichael

Tomorrow God isn't going to ask
What did you dream?
What did you think?
What did you plan?
What did you preach?
He's going to ask, **what did you do?**

—Michel Quoist[4]

CHAPTER TWO

HOW IT ALL BEGAN

There is a first faith and a second faith.

The first faith is the easy, traditional belief of childhood, taken from other people, believed because it belongs to the time and land.

The second faith is the personal conviction of the soul. It is the heart knowing because God has spoken to it.

—Phillip Brooks[5]

What would make a couple in their early fifties, who by normal standards should take a more conservative approach to life—planning for a safe retirement—instead, risk everything to launch a humanitarian venture, when they had no idea of what exactly they were going to do?

For Bob and Char Pagett, the stage was set for this at an early age. Neither Bob nor Char came from wealthy homes. Both came from families not very far above the poverty line. Char's father was a carpenter in San Jose, California; Bob's father was a bookkeeper in Grand Junction, Colorado. Both sets of parents had gone through the Great Depression of the 1930s.

"Most of the time income was hand to mouth," Char said. "But even though there was not much money, we always had a roof over our heads and food on the table." While Char remembers her household as poor, she also remembers that her parents had taken in a sixteen-year-old boy who had run away from an abusive home and needed a place to stay. That concrete act of compassion for those needing help was a graphic example of how she was raised. Char saw firsthand what it meant to help others. Char's two uncles were missionaries, one to Africa and one to Argentina; and as a child Char would help her mother pack boxes with canned foods and other supplies to send to her missionary uncles and their families. Early on, she experienced the rewarding sense of fulfillment in a life of service.

Bob's life was not much different. "We lived in a small house in Grand Junction, Colorado with no refrigerator, just an ice box on the front porch," he said. "My daily job in the winter was to make trips to the basement and break up chunks of coal to feed to the furnace." He was taught early on about having a strong work ethic and doing things the right way the first time. If repairs were needed at the family home, the work was done by Bob's dad with the help of his older son Darrel and young Bob. The Pagett home was open to ministers and missionaries, and as a young child, Bob heard missionary stories.

One thing both families had in common was a deep love for God. Both families attended their respective churches every Sunday, and both were deeply influenced by the Bible's message of loving others and reaching out to those more vulnerable than they.

"While I was in high school, a missionary visited our church. Paul Bruton was a dynamic speaker who talked about his work in

Africa," Bob said. "And that's when I responded to an invitation to come down to the altar and dedicate my life. As I was praying, a song was being played on the piano, '*I'll go where you want me to go, Dear Lord. I'll be what you want me to be.*' At that time, I felt a call to missions, but had no idea how that might play out."

Sadly, in May of 1956, tragedy struck the Pagett family. One month before Bob's high school graduation, his father passed away of heart failure. It was a devastating loss for the family. Bob would no longer have his dad's wisdom at the age of seventeen, at a critical stage of life. His twin sister Bette would not have her father walk her down the aisle during her upcoming wedding. "You're now head of this house," his mother told him. Their lives were upended. Bob had two full-ride college scholarships that he could have accepted, but if he left home after graduation his mother would be alone. So he decided to give up the scholarship and attend the local junior college in Grand Junction. As Bob looks back on that time, he realizes that if he had taken the scholarship, he would not have met Char.

It was about the same time that Char's father decided to take a risk and move his family to Colorado, where a friend had told him of construction opportunities surrounding the uranium boom happening there—a mineral needed to produce atomic energy.

Moving from her familiar surroundings in California, sixteen-year-old Char was devastated to leave her high school, church, and friends. Little did she realize how this move would transform her life and bring her to the man who would become her life partner.

In Colorado, she and Bob met at the local church and soon discovered they had similar interests. Bob played trumpet in the high school band and the local city orchestra and was in line to receive the John Philp Sousa Band Award and other scholarships. Char also played in the school orchestra and later in the city symphonic orchestra, playing the bass violin and piano. In church, Char accompanied Bob on the piano as he played the trumpet. Before long, Bob and Char began dating.

Char and Bob remember a New Year's Evening service at church that seemed to be a life-defining moment for them. As they were leaving the church, an elderly woman slipped and fell on the icy sidewalk in front of them. They knew she was severely injured and took her to the hospital. They called their parents and told them they would stay with the lady until her injury was diagnosed and she was in a hospital bed. It was around 2 a.m. when they finally left the hospital. Char invited Bob into their home where she made toasted cheese sandwiches and soup, and they talked until 4 a.m. Bob saw a depth about Char, her dedication to God and compassion for people. It also didn't hurt that she made the best soup and sandwich Bob had ever had! Bob thought he found the girl for him.

It was on a Sunday afternoon drive in Bob's 1947 Chevy to the Southern Colorado mountains above the town of Ouray, on what is called the Million Dollar Highway, dynamited out of sheer cliffs. Bob found a pullout and stopped the car. Looking across the canyon at a cable that would ferry miners across the deep canyon to a copper mine, Bob said, "I would go hand over hand on that cable across this canyon to prove how much I love you." Thankfully, Char did not put Bob through that test. But there on the canyon side Bob proposed marriage. Char said yes, if Bob would ask her father for her hand in marriage. Since Char's father had married her mother when she was sixteen, it was logical that he would agree to Bob's desire to marry his daughter. Bob recalls that when he asked Char's father for her hand in marriage, he asked, "How would you like to get rid of a boarder?" To which his soon-to-be-father-in-law joked, "Okay, you can have Bill."

Yes, they were young. Very young. Bob was eighteen, Char was seventeen. Bob says, "The death of my father made me realize even more that I wanted to be involved in things that had eternal value." After Bob's first year of junior college and Char's graduation from high school, they were married in their local church in Grand Junction, Colorado on June 7, 1957. A scripture that was meaningful to them is Romans 8:28 (KJV): "And we know that all things work together for good to them that love God, to them who are the called according to His purpose."

They knew God was calling them, only from now on it would not be separate journeys, but a journey of hope together. Their destiny was set. Two high school kids ending up in the same town in Colorado, in the same church, and the same high school. Two kids who found a common bond, both sensing a call to some unknown work of service they both phrased as "a call to missions," who fell in love and couldn't wait to get married.

After a brief honeymoon, they packed up what possessions they had, and with a small trailer Bob had purchased for $75 hitched to his newly acquired 1949 Ford sedan, they headed west for Bethany Bible College in Scotts Valley, California.

Risk was not unfamiliar to this couple. Char's father had risked everything to move to Colorado, with little in his pocket. And Bob's widowed mother was working as a clerk in a garment shop to provide for her daily needs. Bob had worked since he was eleven, buying his own school clothes and at sixteen buying his own car.

"The risk factor was a part of our DNA," Char said. "When we left Colorado right after our wedding to attend Bethany Bible College in California, we had $350 in our pocket and thought we were fine. I think the risk element was already a part of our lives."

"Risk" can be another word for faith. The spiritual teachings that Bob and Char learned early in their lives strongly emphasized what it meant to live by faith. From the time she was a small child, Char remembers in times of crisis or when work for her father was scarce, he would say, "Well, we'll just trust the Lord to provide." Char said, "And God always did provide for us."

Believe Your Beliefs; Doubt Your Doubts

Big leaps of faith often start with steps of faith. Sometimes very, very small steps. And yet the more we step in the right direction, the more exciting life can be, if we are trusting God to lead us.

There are places in all our lives where we look back and see risks of faith that eventually define who we are, who we become. Where we go to college (if we do). What occupation we assume. Whom we marry. Our friends. Most of all, our life values and beliefs—what we stand for, and what becomes most important to us.

Bob and Char believed God was leading them as they chose early marriage and going to Bible college, with Char working while Bob went to college. Looking back on those early years, Char said, "Even though we were young, we had a determination to serve God in any capacity. It meant lots of hard work and very little sleep at times. And sometimes we would have Campbell's Soup for two weeks at a time because we didn't have money for groceries."

When Bob graduated, they chose to leave California to accept an opportunity to a youth pastorate in Oregon—again, with not much money but with high hopes and faith in God that they could make a difference. Most of all, they chose to trust God with what they had and who they were, believing that God would lead them as they set out to make a difference in the world. Char remembers, "God provided safety, provisions for food, and finances. It was an exciting and hard time as we learned to walk by faith."

Bob and Char have a plaque on their wall: "Believe Your Beliefs; Doubt Your Doubts." Faith carried them early on and carries them still. Big leaps of faith take exercise, starting with small steps. Testing. Trusting. And then walking it out.

Dark Moments

> *Sorrow makes deep scars; it writes its record ineffaceably on the heart which suffers. We never get over our great griefs; we are never altogether the same after we have passed through them as we were before. Yet there is a humanizing and fertilizing influence in sorrow. . . . God has ordered that in pressing on. . . we shall find the truest, richest comfort for ourselves.*
>
> **—J. R. Miller**[6]

For the next thirty years following their marriage, Bob and Char had good and busy years in ministry as pastors, youth pastors, music ministers, and state youth directors, in various places in both Oregon and California. There were wonderful and productive years. There were also difficult years.

After they moved to Oregon, Bob and Char's family began to grow. Michelle was born first; then two years later, Cheri joined the family. When Michelle and Cheri were seven and five, Bob and Char had a third daughter, Pamela Renee. But while working as youth directors for their denomination in Oregon, three-month old Pamela suddenly died while they were in Hawaii.

Bob explains, "I was invited to Hawaii to speak to youth on various islands. On a whim, I decided to sell one of our cars and use that money to take the whole family with me to

Hawaii. Our lives were always so busy with very little time for vacation, and this was our first time to really get away with our children, Michelle, Cheri, and Pamela, our three-month-old baby. We were having a wonderful time. We had gone to a restaurant as a family and while the girls were finishing their dinner, Char left to go back to the hotel to nurse Pamela. I planned to stay with the girls and then we would take one final stroll on the beaches of Waikiki. There was a full moon out and it was a beautiful evening.

"As I got back to the hotel and opened the door to our room, I realized we were in a terrible crisis. Pamela had just quit breathing. We didn't know why. I took her from Char and tried to pat her on the back and gave her mouth-to-mouth resuscitation. We desperately called the hotel desk to get a doctor and I took the baby and ran down the fire escape to the hotel lobby where a doctor and a nurse were on vacation. They also began working on our baby girl. The ambulance came and Char and I were whisked to the Kaiser hospital with Pamela Renee while Michelle and Cheri were kept at the hotel with a babysitter. We waited at the hospital for a couple of hours as they tried to resuscitate Pamela, to no avail. Without doubt, it was the darkest day of our lives."

The devastation of losing their baby daughter was something Bob and Char could hardly bear. Char remembers, "During those dark days I felt like my prayers were not being answered, not going any higher than the ceiling. After another sleepless night of asking God, 'Why?', I had a distinct thought, I believe from the Holy Spirit: *Char, I'm here to comfort you but you have to accept that comfort just as you accepted salvation.*

"It was a turning point for me because I realized that my will was involved. I could choose to let this experience embitter me and turn me away from God. Or I could allow it to deepen me and draw me closer to God. It renewed my hope in heaven. For both myself and Bob it was like suddenly, a part of us was in heaven. I identified in a new way. Heaven was no longer an ethereal place that I dreamed about and talked about, but suddenly it became very real."

Matt Sudfeld, one of Bob and Char's grandsons and a graduate of Brown University, worked for Assist International. His mother is Michelle, Bob and Char's oldest daughter, who vividly remembers at age seven the trauma of losing her baby sister Pamela. Recently Matt told us, "I have learned so much from my grandparents by how they handled tragedy. I mean, there's nothing that could be more tragic or torturous than having your baby daughter die in your arms. The most unimaginable pain that a parent can experience. And what so profoundly moves me is that I'm sure my grandparents, to this day, don't know why. And I'm sure they've asked that question a million times. But they stayed true to each other and to God. And when I imagine myself in that situation, I don't know if I would have the courage to face up with God and wrestle with it.

"But instead, they took their pain and their scars in their brokenness, and with God's help turned it into something incredibly beautiful all these years later," Matt said. "And now, it's almost like God did crazy surgery on Bob and Char's hearts and they have this superhuman ability to love all these orphans and vulnerable children across the world. It's like these thousands of vulnerable children are loved by them like their own daughter."

Unfortunately, life didn't get easier for Bob and Char after Pamela's death. After the funeral, Char contracted a virus that attacked her lungs with an infection so severe that she could hardly breathe. It was a five-year saga of trying medications, heavy antibiotics, and cortisone, with nothing seeming to help. She was tied to a machine with treatments every three hours, twenty-four hours a day, doing breathing treatments. Life was very bleak for them during this time.

The life of faith can often be mysterious, perplexing. But adversity can give us a deeper understanding of the mysteries of God and develop in us greater compassion. J. W. Follette wrote,

> The one who has had but little trouble in life is not a particularly helpful person. But one who has gone through a hundred and one trials, experiences, deaths, blasted hopes, shocks, and a tragedy or two and has learned. . . . Such a person is worthwhile. He can enter the need of suffering humanity and pray it through. He can enter perfect fellowship with a person who is in unspoken agony of spirit and pressure of trial. He can look beyond the frailty of flesh and, remembering we are but dust, to trust God with a sublime faith for victory and power. Do not be afraid of the process. I see such rich possibilities in it all. We long to be of service to needy mankind. Nothing can better equip us than to break in spirit and heart and so become clear, sparkling wine, rich and refreshing.[7]

A Change of Plans

Philanthropist Nettie McCormick said, "We plan—and God steps in with another plan for us and he is all-wise and the most loving friend we have, always helping us."[8]

It is a mystery why certain things happen, but sometimes a closed door means an open door to something else. Bob says, "Char's illness put our plans for the future in missions on hold. It made us wonder about the commitment we'd made to be involved with missions. So, my prayer changed: *Lord, if we cannot go to the mission field, then open the door for us to pastor a church where we can have a church with a mission's heart.* I'd read about Oswald J. Smith, the pastor of People's Church in Toronto, who was well known around the world as a pastor at home who traveled overseas and supported many couples out of his church who became full-time missionaries. It was during that time that we received an invitation to pastor a church in Santa Cruz, California."

Bob and Char accepted the invitation to pastor in Santa Cruz, and Char's health gradually became better. A local internist helped her get off the medications, and through his help and God's healing touch Char's health was restored. Bob and Char began an exciting and challenging time of pastoral ministry in Santa Cruz, holding civic auditorium outreaches, as well as feeding programs for the needy in their area. The church developed a mission program and began doing overseas projects, with Bob taking men and women from the church to build churches, schools, etc., across the world. In their seventeen years of pastoring, these trips involved hundreds of their people doing about twenty-five projects overseas. It seemed that God was answering Bob and Char's prayers to pastor a thriving missionary church. However, they faced an incredible amount of adversity as the church tried to relocate and build a bigger facility. They had purchased a beautiful piece of property, but between political petitions and environmental problems they were stymied.

The life of faith is not always an easy walk. Living by faith is directly associated with risk, because with both we must trust in what we cannot always see, touch, know, or feel. It is a reality that is there for us, but just behind the curtain of what we can see. Jesus told his disciples, "If you have faith as small as a mustard seed, you can say to this mountain, 'Move from here to there,' and it will move. Nothing will be impossible for you" (Matt. 17:20). And the Old Testament is filled with stories of people who took huge risks to obey God and fulfill the promises that God had given.

King Solomon wrote these words for the entrepreneurial-spirited:

> Ship your grain across the sea; after many days you may receive a return. Invest in seven ventures, yes, in eight; you do not know what disaster may come upon the land. If clouds are full of water, they pour rain on the earth. Whether a tree falls to the south or to the north, in the place where it falls, there it will lie. Whoever watches the wind will not plant; whoever looks at the clouds will not reap. As you do not know the path of the wind, or how the body is formed in a mother's womb, so you cannot understand the work of God, the Maker of all things. Sow your seed in the morning, and at evening let your hands not be idle, for you do not know which will succeed, whether this or that, or whether both will do equally well. (Eccl. 11:1–6)

Bob and Char grew up learning and believing scriptures like these. And while their lives were not without the testing of their faith and the pain of great loss, what they did know was that "without faith it is impossible to please God" (Heb. 11:6). And that ultimately, there were good plans for them—"plans to give. . . hope and a future" (Jer. 29:11).

We all operate by faith. We have faith that the sun will come up tomorrow, or that when we flip the switch the light will come on. We have faith that when we get in our car, it will start. We use faith to pledge fidelity to our spouses when we marry. We have faith in our leaders and institutions. We live by common types of faith every day. And yet, there are deeper types of faith that challenge us in profound ways and force us to choose a path for which we may not know the outcome.

Two Types of Faith

1. Trusting Faith

One type of faith listed in the Bible is what we might call a "Job-type" of faith. Job was a man who not only served God but was blessed by God. The Bible tells us that one day Satan and God had a conversation. When God expressed his pleasure with Job and his faithfulness, Satan scoffed, "Why shouldn't he when you pay him so well? You have always protected him and his home and his property from all harm. You have prospered everything he does—look how rich he is! No wonder he 'worships' you! But just take away his wealth, and you'll see him curse you to your face!" (See Job 1:9–11).

God agreed to allow Satan to test Job's faith. In the process, Job lost his wealth, his health, his family, and pretty much everything but his own life. Job had no idea why he was going through his great loss and suffering. He was not privy to the conversation between God and Satan. Job was a righteous man, and even though his friends tried to get him to repent, he knew he was right before God. He didn't know why he was hurting; he just knew that he was. Yet he had a stubborn faith: "Though he slay me, yet will I trust him" (Job 13:15, KJV).

One "faith lesson" to be taken from that story is that sometimes we have no clue as to why we are going through a dark place in life. Like Bob and Char's tragedy with their daughter, and Char's health issues, at times our faith is tested as to whether we will "curse God and die" as Job's wife said he should do (Job 2:9, KJV), or if our faith in God will hold us while in the darkness of adversity, even when we cannot understand why.

2. Obedient Faith

This type of faith could be illustrated when God called Noah to build an ark. He gave Noah specific instructions on what to do: the dimensions, the materials, and why he needed to build it. God told Noah to gather the animals and that there would be a flood. Noah knew exactly what he had to do, even though it must have seemed like an enormous assignment. Noah needed big faith for a big job.

Noah's first reaction must have been, "Are you kidding me?" It must have seemed like God was asking Noah to do the impossible. Noah was told not only what to do, but how he should do it.

Knowing what God wants us to do can seem even more frightening than not knowing what God is up to. Noah-type of faith asks if we have the courage to go through with what God is telling us to do—a faith that we can accomplish the task before us, a faith that the resources will be provided, faith that we can get it done in God's timing.

Bob and Char needed both Job-type faith to trust God no matter their circumstances, and Noah-type faith to be obedient to what they felt God was saying to them at different points in their lives. Job-type faith took them through the death of their daughter and Char's illness. Noah-type faith allowed them to start Assist International and to continue for these past thirty years in project after project.

When the book of Hebrews tells us that "without faith it is impossible to please God" (11:6), it reminds us that not only do we need to have faith that the sun will come up tomorrow, but to have a fruitful and productive life. We cannot let adversity sidetrack us, taking us into doubt and despair. We can also have the faith that our lives can count for something bigger than what we may ask or think. God has a plan for us in all of it, in the dark adversities as well as in the amazing plans, talents, and gifts he has given us.

None of us know why God allowed Bob and Char's infant daughter to die. None of us know why God allows millions of children in poorer countries of the world to suffer from hunger and disease. But having hope in these dark places can then lead us to exciting "Noah-type" opportunities. Bob and Char were able to take that tragic experience and turn it into a chance to do something far beyond what they thought they could do for the world's most vulnerable.

And God prepares all of us for what he calls us to do. Whatever our talents, our passion, our interests—if we allow God to work in our life, he will show us the way. We can trust him, knowing that he does all things well. Philip Neri, an Italian priest in the 1500s, wrote, "Cast yourself into the arms of God and be very sure that if He wants anything of you, He will fit you for the work and give you strength."[9] That timeless truth that has not changed in centuries. From the time we are born, God has a plan for us.

Bob said, "Love always results in action. When you love God, he teaches you that loving him means loving others. Sometimes, love causes you to be put in dangerous situations. Sometimes love causes you to put your safety at risk. Love results in selflessness. Instead of thinking about yourself, all you can think about is, *they're in need and I must help.* It's not about me; it's about the most vulnerable and poor in this world."

That passion for those in need had carried them through their years of pastoral ministry but was about to explode into something far more than they could have ever imagined. It was when Bob was a pastor in Santa Cruz, California that both Bob and Char began to feel restless, and that God had a change in store for their lives. But neither they, their family, nor close friends could have imagined what would eventually come to pass.

CHAPTER THREE

CLOSED DOORS—OPEN DOORS

If knowing answers to life's questions is absolutely necessary to you, then forget the journey. You will never make it, for this is a journey of unknowables.

—Madame Jeanne Guyon[10]

Bob and Char pastored the church in Santa Cruz, California for seventeen eventful and productive years, and the church grew in size and scope. But there were also frustrations. Bob explains, "The church was landlocked in a small downtown location which was hampering its growth, and during our last ten years at the church, we tried diligently to relocate. I prayed daily that God would provide a way. But time and again, as we found potential property, Santa Cruz County denied our request."

The adversity seemed relentless, and Bob's life was even threatened on a few occasions. Due to all the public hearings, the church increased in visibility and influence in the community. Despite meeting the necessary requirements for the permits, which included expensive environmental impact reports and enlisting attorneys and engineers (not to mention thousands of dollars), their requests were denied. Since Bob belonged to Rotary and was a charter member of his local group, he developed relationships that were leading to new avenues of service outside the walls of his church, as he got involved in the community and business world. The relationships Bob was forming would prove to be important ones in the years to come. And as Bob looked back on what would later happen through Assist International, his experiences with adversity and the practical experience of learning to speak articulately in city councils and planning commissions would serve him well in the future. As Joel Osteen observed, "Nothing in life has happened to you. It's happened for you. Every disappointment. Every wrong. Even every closed door has helped make you into who you are."[11]

During this time, Bob was able to invite the *Anastasis* to the Santa Cruz harbor. The *Anastasis* is one of the Mercy Ships, a humanitarian organization which provides well-equipped ships functioning as modern hospitals which provide medical help for the most vulnerable in various ports of the world. Bob went to endless meetings and completed stacks of paperwork to gain approval to allow the ship to harbor in Monterey Bay next to the Santa Cruz Wharf, and it was exciting to see the community's response when the *Anastasis* came to Santa Cruz. More than 30,000 people from the area were able to tender out to visit the ship. Thousands of people came: service groups, Rotary members, church people, schools, and many from the community boarded the *Anastasis* to learn more about the Mercy Ships. Ultimately Don Fultz, the chamber of commerce president and Rotary member, was able to get a Rotary grant for $180,000 for operating equipment for the *Anastasis*.

Having the *Anastasis* in Santa Cruz resulted in good will and publicity, and even though Bob was establishing positive relationships in the community, the church was still denied permits to relocate to accommodate their growing needs. Those who had been elected to the County Planning Commission were not philosophically in tune with the church's desire to expand. The closed doors to their church expansion had been relentless for ten discouraging years and it eventually became apparent to Bob that no matter how well planned their relocation presentation would be, it would be denied. Bob remembers, "It took months and months each time to try to gain the city's approval. It was when we were turned down for the third and last time that I lost hope of relocating."

Unanswered Prayers

Reflecting on that time, Bob quotes a Garth Brooks country song: "Sometimes I thank God for unanswered prayers. . . . That just because He doesn't answer doesn't mean He don't care. Some of God's greatest gifts are unanswered prayers."[12] He adds, "Looking back, there would probably be no Assist International if God had answered my prayers for relocating the church. God had a different plan for us. I thank God for that unanswered prayer."

Being stuck on one side of a closed door can certainly be frustrating. In Genesis we read that God promised Abram and Sarai a son, with many descendants, but years went by with no answer. We too can feel trapped, thinking, *this is just my lot in life*. We may try to make things happen in our own way and our own timing, which can only complicate matters. Or something unexpected happens to crush our dreams, and we resign ourselves to what is, instead of believing what can be. We can be tempted to give up.

But how rewarding it is to eventually see that in some circumstances what was *our disappointment* becomes *God's appointment*.

Change of Direction

The walk of faith is often an obscure one. We wonder when to persist despite obstacles to achieve a dream. And we wonder when we must let go of what we are pursuing and instead go a different direction. It was during the time of knocking on what seemed to be closed doors for the Pagetts' dream of expanding their church that Bob and Char had an experience that changed the trajectory of their lives.

In 1989, Nancie and I (Bill) invited them on a trip to the International Book Fair, which was to be held in Moscow that year. I was a member of the board of the Evangelical Christian Publishers Association, and we were excited about the privilege of helping man the booth at the Moscow Book Fair where we and some other Christian publishers were going to give away ten thousand copies of the Bible translated into the Russian contemporary language. At the time, Bob was on the board of our publishing company, and we wanted to include him and Char in this historic outreach.

It was an unprecedented time of upheaval in Eastern Europe and the Soviet Union. Ronald Reagan was president of the United States and Mikhail Gorbachev was head of the Soviet Union. *Glasnost* and *perestroika* (meaning "openness" and "reconstruction") were new concepts that were beginning to allow political and social reform that would eventually bring down the Berlin Wall and end the Cold War. It also brought us an opportunity to attend the Moscow Book Fair to pass out a new Russian translation of the Bible.

We first flew to Vienna, Austria, where the four of us rented a car that would take us to Budapest, Hungary for a flight to Moscow, the cheapest way to get there. Hungary had just "punched a hole" in the Iron Curtain and East Germans were pouring into Hungary.

As we drove toward Budapest, we saw the Red Cross tents that were set up to house and feed thousands of East Germans crossing the Hungarian border, who were fleeing communism and on their way to West Germany. We watched breaking news happen before our eyes, astounded at seeing history being made.

At the Moscow Book Fair in the Exposition Center, where the four of us along with some other Christian publishers were assigned to pass out Bibles, people not only lined the building to receive one of those ten thousand Bibles, but the line stretched outside for almost a half-mile. It was an exhilarating experience to place the Bibles in eagerly outstretched hands. Many people, some with tears in their eyes, received their copies reverently. Of the six hundred booth displays present—including booths by Madelyn Murray O'Hair, representing American atheists—it was only the Bible booth that attracted this magnitude of attention. There were so many people pressing to get their way through to our booth to receive the Bibles that the military guard had to be brought in to bring order. It was surreal. We couldn't help but think of how many Bibles we all had at home, in various versions, and we realized what a rare privilege it was to be part of this historic moment.

At the time Doug Ross, executive director of the Evangelical Christian Publishers Association, said in an interview with the *LA Times*, "We finally felt the time was right and no one would get in trouble for distributing the Bibles." Ross recalls, "One man begged me for a Bible, but I didn't have any more for that day, so I had to say no. He looked me in the eyes and said in English, 'Maybe you will remember me.' I think that's important," Ross added. "We should all remember him. We in the United States, where everybody has a Bible on the shelf, have to remember that in the Soviet Union, there are many people who can't see a Bible, hold a Bible, read a Bible."[13]

"It was one of the most incredible times of our lives," Bob said. "Thousands of people came to receive a Bible and when the Bibles were all gone, more people still came." Bob and Char, along with others manning the booth, took an additional 17,000 names and addresses of those who still wanted a Bible. And it was Bob and Char's church in Santa Cruz that committed to mail the Bibles to these thousands of Russians after the exposition was over.

After Bob and Char returned home, something had changed for them. Their world in Santa Cruz seemed too small. One day, a close friend of Bob's who owned auto dealerships in the Bay Area asked Bob if he would join him for lunch.

As the conversation progressed, Bob excitedly told his friend of his recent trip to the Soviet Union. His friend listened for a while, and then replied, "Bob, I sense you are planning to leave your pastorate." Bob was taken back as he and Char had privately discussed this, trying to decide if it was the right move for them. His friend then said, "Tell me your vision, what you want to do with your life."

Bob hesitated, as he was still unsure about what to say. Then the words tumbled out, "I want to start a humanitarian organization that will be directed to Eastern Europe, now that the Iron Curtain is falling." The surprising statement coming from his lips was a first small step in their future, but it was the step of faith he needed to push him forward.

Helen Keller wrote, "When one door of happiness closes, another opens; but often we look so long at the closed door that we do not see the one which has been opened for us." The benefit of a closed door is that it forces us to try other doors. It helps us get outside of our own world. While we don't leave our own "roots," our own identity, we begin to see a network of exciting opportunities calling us to join them or assist them.

In January of 1990, Bob preached a sermon titled "Taking Inventory of Your Life," which reflected Bob and Char's own personal inventory. The theme of that sermon was a scripture from Psalm 119:49, "Remember your word to your servant, for you have given me hope." After the conclusion of Bob's sermon, he read his letter of resignation. Little did Bob and Char realize at the time of preaching that sermon that the hope they felt in moving forward into a new unknown venture with God would bring hope to thousands of others around the world over the next thirty-plus years.

As Oswald Chambers wrote, "We try to make calls out of our own spiritual consecration, but when we are put right with God, He blights all our sentimental convictions and devotional calls. He brushes them all aside, and rivets us with a passion that is terrific to one thing we had never dreamed of, and in the condition of real communion with God, we overhear Him saying, 'Whom shall I send, and who will go for us?' and for one radiant, flashing moment we see what God wants, and say in conscious freedom— 'Here am I, send me.'"[14]

The decision to resign their church set in motion a roller coaster of events for Bob and Char. Resigning their church meant that at fifty-one years of age, Bob would no longer have a salary. He and Char had no specific plans, nor knew exactly what they would do next. All they had was a $30,000 "send-off" offering given to them by the Santa Cruz church they had pastored for seventeen years, and faith that whatever was next would be an exciting venture with God.

"I wrestled a lot with this decision," Char recalls. "But I kept remembering the faces of the people in Moscow and the Red Cross tents as people streamed out of East Germany. And I kept recalling the time when we were boarding the plane to leave Russia, and as the plane lifted off the runway several people cheered and hugged each other. As we flew, we found out that there were several Jewish families on board who were escaping communism with virtually nothing but the clothes they were wearing. Bob and Bill emptied their pockets and gave them all the cash we had remaining," she said. "And while I had some fear about the unknown, I also felt excitement about the possibilities of helping others."

Bob described how that leap of faith felt: "I sometimes felt like we were diving into a swimming pool that may not have any water!" But he went on to say, "The Bible says that the steps of a good person are ordered by the Lord, and I believed he would come alongside, that he would not abandon us."

When asked what he would say to others who were contemplating a leap of faith, Bob answered, "Sometimes you have a spark of a dream and you feel an excitement, a passion—and you think maybe this is God, but maybe it's just a crazy idea. But I've found that every step that we take in the direction of our passion to do something for others, God is there to meet with us."

Sometimes God may be asking us to have patience and to keep knocking on the locked door. But at other times, when one door seems to continue to be slammed shut, another door opens that ignites your passion and calling. It's time to pay attention—to step out in faith. When that happens, it can be God showing you a new direction—which is what happened to Bob and Char.

It must be said here, that just because you take a leap of faith—just because you let go of what you are currently doing to answer your calling more fully in life—it does not mean everything will be smooth sailing. Dreams may not always be fulfilled easily or quickly. There are times of waiting, of not knowing if this really is the way we should go. There are times when answering the call

is not clearly defined. But finding your true calling, while rarely
without some bumps in the road, is always the most rewarding
way to do life.

Dare to Answer the Call

*We're all called. If you're here breathing, you have
a contribution to make to our human community.
The real work of your life is to figure out your function—your part in the whole—as soon as
possible, and then get about the business of fulfilling
it as only you can.*

—Oprah Winfrey[15]

All of us have a calling. Your calling may not be a calling deeply
rooted in faith like Bob and Char's, but all of us have something that we can offer the world—something to give to others.
No life is without meaning. And if we answer the call that will
take us to something bigger or more challenging, we must let go
of where we are. Walking away from what is a closed door can
mean letting go of even good things, or letting go of old dreams,
to embrace the new. It may mean letting go of our securities.
That is the life of faith: We let go to move on—to walk through
another door.

Os Guinness wrote, "Deep in our hearts, we all want to find
and fulfill a purpose bigger than ourselves. Only such a larger purpose can inspire us to heights we could never reach on our own.
For each of us, the real purpose is personal and passionate: to
know what we are here to do, and why."[16]

Rick Warren likewise explains that your heart shows you
your passion—that the thing that you love reveals who you are:

"What I am able to do, God wants me to do. . . . To discover God's will for your life, you should seriously examine what you are good at doing and what you're not good at. If God hasn't given you the ability to carry a tune, he isn't going to expect you to be an opera singer. God will never ask you to dedicate your life to a task you have no talent for. On the other hand, the abilities you do have are a strong indicator of what God wants you to do with your life."[17]

Every person has talents, gifts, strengths. And if a person of faith wants to grow, experiences can show us new doors and how to maximize our God-given talents. Bob and Char's grandson Matt observed this about his grandparents: "The thing about Bob, he has incredible skills at networking. Bob is kind of like the quarterback who knows how to get the best out of every receiver and other players on the team. And he loves to drop back and throw the bomb in hopes of a game-changing score. That's one reason he says 'Yes' to so many projects. He helps everybody work together to better their abilities to accomplish a goal. And Char is so sharp at logistics. When Bob says 'Yes,' she is the one who must figure out the travel plans and how to make it happen. She did this for years before internet or cell phones, arranging the group airline schedules, handling the finances and keeping all the details straight. I have no idea how she did all of this, but these two make a great team. Bob's the visionary, Char is the detail person. There is no way Bob could have done any of this without Char."

Yes to New Experiences

When you feel stuck, sometimes it's good to say yes to a new experience, as new experiences can open the doors to new possibilities. Bob and Char's experience of the trip to Moscow helped them see new things happening in the world, and their place in it. Char says, "That first trip to Eastern Europe gave some focus to our dream and gave us faith to move forward."

Bob and Char experienced the frustration of a closed door. But as they followed their passion and calling, they chose to experience something new, which led to experiencing another, wider door opening. It was a door that would lead to amazing possibilities.

Oswald Chambers said, "Continually restate to yourself what the purpose of your life is. The destined end of man is not happiness, nor health, but holiness. . . . The one thing that matters is whether a man will accept the God who will make him holy."[18]

Donald Clifton and Paula Nelson describe some practical ways that we can understand our calling. They say to "find out what you do well and do more of it." They suggest people look at their natural abilities and things they do that come easily for them. Everyone has that thing he or she does best—the thing that can make one lose track of time when engaged in it, where one really comes alive. It takes simple awareness of one's own self to understand one's calling. From there:

Listen to yearnings. Something deep inside you says, *I'd love to do that! I could do that.*

Watch for satisfaction. Analyze where you experience emotional and psychological rewards. When you are doing this, you feel a sense of satisfaction.

Watch for rapid learning. If you catch on to something easily, you're likely to be good at it. What kind of projects or work energizes you? That is most likely an indication of your strength.[19]

And then, of course, listen to God! What is he calling us to do or be? It is not a fight, or a struggle. He uses us just as we are, with our own unique gifts and talents.

The Call to Make a Difference

Divine open doors are not for the arrogant, adulterers
and wasters, they are only meant for the humble that
will be wise with the opportunity and blessing that
comes from them.

—Bamigboye Olurotimi, Lagos, Nigeria

The call to make a difference may start with a dream, a burning passion. From the time Bob and Char Pagett were young, they burned with the dream of making a difference—that helping people was their God-given calling. Vision carries us forward. The writer of Proverbs noted, "Where there is no vision, the people perish" (Prov. 29:18, KJV). And we can nourish those dreams of ours. James Allen wrote, "Dream lofty dreams, and as you dream, so shall you become. . . . Dreams are the seedlings of realities."[20] Keeping a vision starts with believing that with God's strength and guidance, we can persist in finding open doors to live our calling.

A good question to ask ourselves is: What motivates us to fulfill our calling? It is essential to understand the difference between our *ego driving* us versus our *calling inspiring* us. Ego is more self-centered and can drive us toward selfish goals such as fame, wealth, and accumulation of things. While these goals are not bad in themselves, they are temporary. Calling has more to do with listening to the inner voice of God whisper to us that He has a divine purpose for our talents and abilities to help change the world around us. And we can help carry out His purpose of love and mercy and justice.

Author Frederick Buechner says that your calling is "the place where your deep gladness meets the world's deep need."[21] Your ego might help you function in life, but it is your calling that provides a more genuine and purposeful expression of your life.

The psalmist wrote eloquently of how God creates us: "Oh yes, you shaped me first inside, then out; you formed me in my mother's womb. You know exactly how I was made, bit by bit, how I was sculpted from nothing into something. Like an open book, you watched me grow from conception to birth; all the stages of my life were spread out before you, the days of my life all prepared before I'd even lived one day" (Ps. 139:13–14, MSG).

Char said, "Compassion has to come from the heart. If you care about people, it's easy. But if all your life is inwardly focused and all you care about is having the right clothes and having beautiful furniture or a fancy car, there is little room for compassion." She went on to say, "There are so many people who are trapped with an inward focus. But when we take them on some of our trips to see how the most vulnerable are just barely coping to stay alive, it opens their eyes and compassion creeps in. I cannot tell you how many people who have gone on a trip with us express, *it changed my life.*" Experiences can change your life and open your eyes to new open doors.

Compassion helps us see beyond ourselves. Bob Pierce, founder of World Vision prayed, "Let my heart be broken by the things that break the heart of God." That is a risky prayer. But it's a big and powerful one.

Jim Stunkel served as a battalion chief with the fire department in San Jose, California while volunteering on humanitarian trips with Assist. As he experienced how lives of people were changed by the simple and profound act of meeting their needs, his life was changed too. After seventeen years as a volunteer, Bob recruited Jim to be vice president and director of operations at A.I., and subsequently also the general manager of A.I. Medical

Oxygen Production PLC in Ethiopia. Jim told us, "I began as a part-time volunteer, and the rewards exceeded my expectations. One life that is saved can in turn save many more, and when one partner joins the work, that partner can bring others as well. There will be challenges, but a great truth is also magnified, as Jesus said, 'He who finds his life will lose it, and he who loses his life for my sake will find it.'"

How do you know when to keep knocking on a door? To be sure, at times one must be persistent for good things to happen. Persistence pays. But there are also times when a door is clearly shut. We turn to another door. Another possibility. And a new way opens.

When Bob and Char saw one door close and looked with excitement to a door that God was opening, they had no idea that this new venture would take them places they could not imagine, nor of the dangers and challenges they would face.

If human love does not carry a man beyond himself,
it is not love. If love is always discreet, always wise,
always sensible and calculating, never carried beyond
itself, it is not love at all.

—Oswald Chambers[22]

CHAPTER FOUR

EMBRACING THE CHALLENGE

The difference between world changers and stagnant drifters comes down to the ability to focus on opportunities, and then seize them.

—Drenda Keesee [23]

By now, Bob and Char were passionately committed to the concept of helping meet needs in Eastern Europe. How exactly that was to play out was not yet clear, but they knew with building excitement that there was no turning back. They saw a pressing challenge, and they were willing to see what they could do.

As Nancie and I were doing research for this book, we thought of our trip with Bob and Char to work the Christian Publisher booth at the Moscow Book Fair in 1989. It was a historic moment. As previously mentioned, we drove a car from Austria into Budapest, Hungary, because it offered the best flights into Moscow.

The four of us watched hundreds of people stream from East Germany into Hungary. Red Cross tents were set up and volunteers were giving them food, medical help, and a few supplies. I (Nancie) remember wondering with growing alarm, "What's wrong with us? Why are we heading east when everyone else is heading west?" But head east we did, into the Eastern communist bloc countries, while many desperate people were escaping to the West.

This is a classic example of what Bob and Char have done since beginning Assist International. Confronted with a need, instead of avoiding it (as many of us would do!) they embraced it and saw an opportunity to help the most vulnerable.

Opportunity within Crisis

The question is not what you look at but what you see.

—Henry David Thoreau

As we write, we are amid a global pandemic and while there is much to fear and much to learn, as many on the front lines of medicine and scientific research are discovering important data to help make effective vaccines and treatments to deal with novel viruses. So, despite this moment of crisis, there is opportunity. We tend to see crises as something fearful, something to get past, or at least avoid (and indeed, they are). However, history shows us that crises can be powerfully instructive places as we look for solutions.

Many great organizations and movements were birthed out of a crisis. The Red Cross was started by Clara Barton during the terrible carnage of the Civil War. Mothers Against Drunk Driving (MADD) was begun by a woman after her teenaged daughter was killed by a drunk driver. President John F. Kennedy said, "The Chinese use two brush strokes to write the word 'crisis.' One brush stroke stands for danger: the other for opportunity. In a crisis, be aware of the danger—but recognize the opportunity."[24] During a crisis, incentives and motivations change, potentially leading to new cooperative behaviors and even to the creation of new systems or structures.

What is our response to a challenge? Do we try to escape? Take the easy way out? Deny it exists? Amazing things can happen as we move toward it—especially at God's direction. A crisis can offer great possibilities.

The story is told in the Bible of Moses's challenge to lead his people to the Promised Land. They finally escaped from Egypt only to face the Red Sea—a seemingly impossible obstacle, as Pharaoh's army was in hot pursuit behind them. What were they to do? God told Moses to stretch out his rod over the Red Sea and lead the people through it. As he did so, the seas parted, and Moses led his people on over to the other side. When Pharaoh's armies came after them, the seas closed over them, and the people were saved. The Red Sea—an impossible challenge—became their means of rescue. They were saved by heading *into* the obstacle, instead of running from it. God has a way of turning challenges into triumphant opportunities, as Bob and Char were discovering.

The Birth of Assist International

Every castle was once started with a single block;
despise no small beginnings.

—Israelmore Ayevor[25]

When Bob and Char knew they were in a time of transition, they met with their daughters and sons-in-law. After a family dinner, Bob and Char shared with their family their dream to form a not-for-profit organization. Together they had a brainstorming session, and Tim Reynolds finally came up with "Assist International." Things were starting to take shape.

By now Bob was carefully watching news reports about the drastic changes taking place in Eastern Europe. From their recent trip to the Moscow Book Fair, he and Char felt an increasing desire to help people in countries who were coming out of oppression under communism. In 1990, not knowing exactly what was needed or how to proceed, they decided to make an exploratory trip to Eastern Europe.

Shortly before they left, they received two phone calls that helped give direction to their trip. One call was from a leader in Christian publishing asking if Bob and Char could try to find leaders of the emerging church in Eastern Europe who could advise them on publishing and literature opportunities to help the churches in Eastern Europe. The other call was from another Christian leader who suggested that Bob try to connect with Dr. Ion V. Patrascu, as there were reports about a dire problem with AIDS in Romania that had been discovered by Dr. Patrascu.

Immense Challenges

In April of 1990, Bob and Char left for Eastern Europe. Char said, "We were not sure where we were going and not sure we could even find the people we needed to see. We simply were trusting God to lead us to the right places and to the right people. We laugh now about how naive we were and the crazy situations we encountered."

They first landed in Sofia, Bulgaria. There they were able to locate some Christian leaders and get information about their literature needs. Their plan was to fly from there to Bucharest, Romania, but discovered there were no planes going from Sofia to

Bucharest. It was almost impossible to get information. Crowds and the chaos of people trying to leave Bulgaria was choking the streets. Finally, they found someone who helped them get tickets on an all-night train to Bucharest, Romania.

"Bob was still dressed in his suit and tie from speaking at a church in Sofia, and I was in high heels and a dress," Char said. "We boarded a train crammed not only with people, but chickens, goats, and various other items, not to mention lots of bottles of wine and whiskey! When we found our assigned sleeping compartment, there was an intoxicated woman assigned to the same compartment. Since it was an all-night train, Bob was assigned the bottom bunk, I was assigned to the middle bunk, and the drunk woman was on the top bunk. All through the night, she would open the window and toss out empty whiskey bottles."

The next morning, a businessman passing through their car was surprised to see them. He stopped to ask, "What are you doing on this train?" He warned them to be very careful as this was a bad place to be. When departing the train, the kind man helped them find a taxi to a hotel in the center of the city. The cockroach-infested hotel was bullet-ridden, dark, and cold.

The following morning, as Bob and Char emerged from their hotel in Bucharest, they were struck by the desperate needs of people everywhere. The country was in turmoil, and some streets were closed off by students on a hunger strike, demonstrating against the leading candidate to become president—who had been an associate of Ceausescu, the recently executed leader whose powerful oppression and corruption had devastated Romania.

Bob and Char saw international reporters roaming the streets, capturing the stories of devastation and human suffering. Thousands of children, some as young as five years old, were sleeping on the streets and in abandoned buildings. They were begging and foraging on the streets to survive.

At one point, as Bob was walking ahead of Char on the streets, she observed what appeared to be a gang of hoodlums ready to pick Bob's pocket. Fearing they would snatch his wallet and passport, Char screamed out a warning; as Bob turned, they ran away. There were beggars everywhere asking for money.

Bob was introduced to a pastor of a church in Bucharest and was invited by that pastor to speak at his church that evening. After the service, they were warned not to go through the center of town back to their hotel, due to a riot taking place. Tanks were in the streets and people reported gunshots, so the taxi took them through darkened side streets to their hotel.

The army generals who had turned against Ceausescu were attempting to run the country, but critical shortages of everything caused people to be in long lines stretching for several blocks, waiting for a handout of short supplies of food. No one knew what was going to happen as the new government was trying to emerge.

History of Romania

It's important to understand that Romania was not always in a dire condition. Before World War II, Romania was ruled by the benevolent King Carol and had a robust economy. In fact, Romania was known as "the breadbasket of Europe," with rich agriculture, mining resources, and industrial manufacturing that included autos and airplanes. People were prospering, beautiful homes were built, and there was ample food for all.

But during World War II, King Carol of Romania aligned with Hitler and Mussolini, more out of threat of invasion than ideology. Hitler wanted to tap the rich oil fields of Ploesti to help run his war machine, and King Carol knew Hitler would take it by force if he did not give him what he wanted.

But as the war progressed and Hitler continued to invade country after country, the Western allies made an "unholy alliance" with Russia to defeat Hitler, which ultimately turned the tide of war. When King Carol realized what was happening, he switched his allegiance to the West, which now included Russia. In many ways, King Carol was caught between a rock and a hard place. He knew that Stalin coveted Romania, but he hoped that Romania would remain allies of the West after the war. They did not want this war and did not want Nazism or communism, but their world was caught in the middle of it all.

After the war and the negotiations at Yalta where territorial divisions were finalized, Romania came under Stalin and communism. Fearing for his life, King Carol and his family fled to Switzerland. Shortly thereafter, because many tried to flee to the West, the Iron Curtain and the Berlin Wall were constructed.

Oppressive Years for Romania

For decades after the war, the outside world knew little about what was happening in Romania. And what was happening wasn't good. When Nicolai Ceausescu rose from the Communist Party ranks to become the supreme leader of Romania in 1974, he soon became known as one of the most ruthless dictators in all Eastern Europe, totally committed to the communist ideology. Through no choice of the people, Romania became one of the most oppressed nations of the world under communism, eventually becoming a dark and mysterious place to the outside world.

Ceausescu's wife Elena was placed as head of science and technology, even though she had no education or training in either science or technology and had never even attended college. All property was to be turned over to the state. Dissidents, intellectuals, priests, pastors, and property owners who defied the changes disappeared, to be never heard of again, as the black "death van" would come through the neighborhoods. If the person who owned the property would sign over their land to the state, they would survive. Those who refused to sign over their properties were never seen again, many going to prison or put to death.

It was rumored that supreme leader Nicolae Ceausescu had a dream to raise up a huge army. To accomplish this, all married couples were ordered to have at least five children or be penalized. This helps to explain why, after the fall of Ceausescu, Bob and Char saw on the newly liberated streets of Bucharest so many orphans and children roaming the streets. Parents desperate for basic needs had simply been unable to care for their children.

Laws in Romania had been oppressive. Under Ceausescu, no Romanians could have a foreign visitor in their homes. Communist local leaders mixed in the churches to hear the sermons to see if there was anything negative being said against the regime. Sermons had to be reviewed before they were preached. The churches that cooperated with the state were monitored but largely left alone. Some denominational leaders were increasingly being mistrusted by their followers because of their allegiance to Ceausescu. Underground churches formed and dark window blinds were used to keep authorities from seeing people studying the Bible.

Ceausescu took more and more of the country's resources to fund his army and build a massive marble building in honor of himself that he called "Ceausescu's Palace." Nearly the size of the Pentagon, half of the Romanian army was drafted to help build it. To finance this huge project and try to pay cash as the construction took place, food became scarcer for the people as agricultural goods as well as oil and mining resources were exported to bring in more cash. During the winter, the heat was turned off in people's homes to preserve energy resources.

Before 1989, under the regime of Ceausescu, abortion and contraception were banned unless women had given birth to five children. These policies, designed to raise the birth rate, resulted in many infants being abandoned by their parents shortly after birth. Food and energy resources became scarce, and many families struggled to survive. In fear of having their children die of malnutrition or freezing to death in harsh winters, families were tearfully forced to give some of their children to the state-run orphanages where it was rumored there was food and warm shelter. Thousands of children of all ages became orphans or abandoned to live in state-run orphanages. Many of those children fled the horrific conditions to live in the streets.

In August of 1989, the Director of the Institute of Virology (the blood department) of Romania, Dr. Ion V. Patrascu was asked to test the blood of a fourteen-year-old girl in one of the orphanages in Bucharest, the capital city. The medical people thought the girl had leukemia. Dr. Patrascu was shocked when the test showed that she had the HIV/AIDS virus. To confirm what he discovered, he sent the test to a medical group in Paris, France to confirm the test. When the report came back that the girl indeed had the HIV virus, Dr. Patrascu began testing other children in the orphanage and found they all had the virus. Dr. Patrascu shared the results of his tests with the minister of health, who passed the information on to Ceausescu. Ceausescu scoffed at the idea and told the minister of health to tell Patrascu that "there is not an AIDS problem in Romania. AIDS is a Western problem, not a Romanian problem."

To combat the malnutrition and severe anemia of infants in the state-run orphanages, infants were given intravenous injections of untested blood known as microinfusion.[26] This standard practice, which was supposed to boost immunity, ironically left a generation of children with the HIV virus. Approximately ten thousand children in the period 1987–1991, plus a growing number of adults, became infected. No one really knows where the blood came from, but as Dr. Patrascu continued to test more and more children and observe the records of blood infusions, he realized that thousands of orphaned children had, most likely, been infected with AIDS by tainted untested blood injected with unsterilized needles. This was done based on an antiquated belief that blood infusions would boost nutritional and immunological health in young children.

With concern for the welfare of the children, Dr. Patrascu decided to invite a French medical group to Bucharest for a seminar to be held in October 1989, on how to combat the AIDS virus. When Ceausescu found out that Patrascu was going to host a seminar on the problem, the communist Securitate invaded Dr. Patrascu's office, destroyed his blood testing laboratory equipment, and removed him as director of the Department of Virology. Placed under house arrest, he was warned to say nothing and to do no more testing, at the threat of his life. The seminar was cancelled.

While the Romanian people were living in isolation and in utter misery, with their basic human rights violated, things in the broader communist world were changing. Gorbachev was moving the Soviet Union toward more openness. The Iron Curtain was being dismantled, but Ceausescu appeared on Romanian national television and told his people that Romania would forever remain communist. "Down with *glasnost* and down with *perestroika*," he declared.

But political change was coming, and it was also coming to Romania. In Timisoara, at a small Hungarian Reformed Church, Pastor Laszalo Tokes began to publicly criticize Ceausescu in his morning sermons. On December 16, 1989, Ceausescu ordered the Securitate to remove him as pastor of the church.

Pastor Tokes called Peter Dugulescu, Pastor of Bethel Baptist Church of Timisoara, and told him that authorities were coming to remove him as pastor of the church. Members of the Hungarian Reformed Church and members of Bethel Baptist Church gathered at the front door of the building that housed the church and the basement apartment of the pastor and his family. All they had to defend their pastor was each other, as they held lighted candles and sang hymns. When the military showed up to arrest Pastor Tokes and his family and realized they would have to go through this singing and praying gauntlet to get to the pastor, they hesitated.

While this was happening, Bethel Church was having a series of youth services with a guest pastor, not far from the Hungarian Reformed Church. More than 1,500 people were attending the services, and on Saturday night after the service, the young people headed toward the trolley cars to take them home. As coincidence would have it, the trolley station was near the Hungarian Reformed Church, where demonstrators were holding their candlelight vigil.

When the military detachment saw the large crowd of young people headed their way, they assumed they were coming to take part in the vigil. At that moment fire hoses from huge fire trucks began to spray the approaching group with water to disperse them. What began as a peaceful demonstration between the soldiers and the people holding candles in front of the Hungarian Reformed Church suddenly became a political rally. Young people began to demonstrate on the streets of Timisoara. Shots rang out and one girl was killed, others wounded.

All through the night and into the next day, tensions ignited demonstrations, and spread through the city and to other cities, even though the government had shut down radio and television access. In Timisoara, students stood in front of military tanks. Ripping open their shirts they yelled, "Kill me, I would rather die than live under communism!" Other students cut the hammer-and-sickle out of the communist flag and demonstrated on the steps of the Orthodox Church at the far end of Timisoara Square, in the middle of the city. The church doors had been locked and soldiers, under orders, began to shoot at the students who desperately tried to retreat inside the church. They were gunned down while trying to open the locked doors. Many lives were lost as demonstrations went on for several days all over Romania.

Ceausescu then called for a televised rally in Bucharest, where he could speak to the people to squelch the unrest. On the same day he was speaking in Bucharest, an impromptu rally of an estimated 150,000 people took place in Timisoara Square. Timisoara Square in downtown Timisoara is a beautiful square with flowers and shops. At one end of the square is the Orthodox Church; at the other end is the opera house, with a large balcony above its massive doors.

Peter Dugulescu's Challenge at Timisoara Square

The ultimate measure of a man is not where he stands in moments of comfort and convenience, but where he stands at moments of challenge and controversy.

—Martin Luther King, Jr.[27]

In October of 2019, we stood in Timisoara Square with Bob and Char, Ralph and Michelle Sudfeld, and Ligia Dugulescu, daughter of Peter Dugulescu, the famous pastor who stood to speak before the thousands of people at that pivotal moment of history in Romania.

As we walked through the beautiful square, sipping coffees from Starbucks (now in the square, as well as other shops and restaurants), we saw the bullet holes in the buildings that had been left there to remind the people of that dramatic moment of freedom. What a difference thirty years makes!

It was a beautiful fall day, and we listened as Ligia told us the story. She was only a girl when she saw her father rise to the occasion. The political dissidents had called for a pastor to speak before the crowd. It was understood that whoever spoke had to say to the crowd, "Down with Ceausescu" in their speech. Her father Peter Dugulescu, pastor of Bethel Baptist Church, offered to speak, not knowing if he would live long enough to even finish his speech. Ligia told us that tears ran down her cheeks as she watched her father walk up the stairs to the balcony of the opera house. She was terrified of what could happen to him, but so proud of his bravery. Standing on the balcony of the opera house at the far end of Timisoara Square, Peter Dugulescu boldly declared that imprisoned pastors should be released, and that democracy should return to Romania. He shouted out that he hoped to see Bible reading and prayer return to homes and schools. The masses cheered as he spoke. Knowing he could be shot and killed at any moment, he shouted out, "Down with Ceausescu!"

As we stood in the square, reflecting on that dramatic moment, Bob told us, "Peter told me later that he did not know who would be down after that speech, him or Ceausescu." As it turned out, it was Ceausescu. People watching Ceausescu's televised speech taking place in Bucharest saw the crowds there rebelling against Ceausescu who, along with his wife, was forced to flee in a helicopter escaping the communist administration building.

At that same time in Timisoara Square, Peter announced to the 150,000 people that the Ceausescus had fled by helicopter from Bucharest. The people cheered. Then the thousands of people in Timisoara Square turned toward the church at the opposite end of the square and knelt, as Peter led them in the Lord's Prayer. After the prayer, people stood and cheered in unison, "God exists! God exists!"

As history now records, the generals in Romania's army had already decided that things must change. After Ceausescu's helicopter landed, he and his wife were placed in an armored vehicle and taken to an army base outside Bucharest. To their surprise, they were put on trial by a military tribunal for crimes against the people of Romania.

On Christmas day after a two-hour trial, both Ceausescu and his wife were executed by a firing squad. This was announced on national radio and television. The oppressive hold on Romania was broken, and for the first time in fifty years Christmas carols and hymns were heard all over the country. On the radio they said, "Today the spirit of the antichrist is gone, and the spirit of Christ has been resurrected!"

But the massive problems and chaos of Romania would not soon resolve. A new government was being formed and there was promise of elections. But there were still huge shortages of food, as the industrial infrastructure and locally owned farms had been decimated. The economy was in shambles. Dr. Patrascu, who had been reinstated as the head of the Institute of Virology, announced at a press conference the news about the spread of HIV virus among the children in the state-run orphanages.

On Bob and Char's first trip to Romania in 1990, Bob had arranged an appointment with Dr. Patrascu; and at their meeting, Bob was introduced to Dr. Patrascu as the president of Assist International. In Patrascu's view, the name "Assist International" sounded like an impressive organization in California. He did not know that this was a barely started organization that consisted of the two people in front of him, whose office was in a second bedroom of their home equipped with a phone and a fax machine.

Dr. Patrascu shared the story about the huge problem of AIDS and showed them recent articles featuring him in major news sources. He asked if Bob would set up a tour for him in America so that Dr. Patrascu could get support to address the medical problems of Romania.

With a step of faith, Bob agreed to do so.

From Romania, the Pagetts visited Hungary, Czechoslovakia, and Berlin. Everywhere they went they encountered both chaos and excitement—chaos as new governments were being formed and shortages of everything were evident; excitement as people began to see new freedom and opportunity emerging. Berlin was riveted with emotion now that friends and families were being reunited. People were still taking hammers and sledgehammers to break up pieces of the Berlin Wall. Bob and Char were welcomed with joy during this historic moment. Bob was given a chunk of concrete that had been part of the Berlin Wall. He stuffed it in his suitcase and brought it home, as a reminder that tearing down walls of oppression was opening new gateways of hope. But there was much work to be done.

It is important to stress how pivotal Romania was for Bob and Char in the early days of Assist International. The relationships and connections they made, the countless trips to help build orphan homes, the many trips, and the other workers they brought in to help bring medical equipment and supplies literally helped rebuild the infrastructure of Romania. What they began in Romania has shaped the direction and identity of Assist International, which now reaches many other countries around the world.

On their first trip to Romania, Bob and Char were confronted by seeing the enormous challenge; and then, as they embraced the challenge and said yes to helping, they found ways to network and empower others as well to meet Romania's desperate needs.

After Bob and Char returned home from their first trip, Bob began to set up an itinerary for Dr. Ion Patrascu to visit the United States. Bob started by calling his friends in Rotary, his pastor friends, and other contacts he had developed over the years to find places for Dr. Patrascu to present the medical needs of Romania. Eventually, the itinerary consisted of meetings in Chicago, Denver, and the Bay Area near where Bob and Char lived.

Dr. Patrascu arrived in August of 1990 for the series of meetings. Everywhere he went, there were audiences of doctors, medical and hospital administrators, political leaders, and others eager to know more about Romania. In Chicago, where there is a large population of Romanian expatriates, many came to hear more about their former country.

The tour continued in the Bay Area of California, with Dr. Patrascu speaking in hospitals, medical schools, and Rotary clubs. He was on radio talk shows and interviewed on television. The more he spoke, the more the question was asked about who brought him to America for this tour. He would say, "Bob Pagett, president of Assist International."

Bob and Char enlisted family and friends to answer their office phone and take messages. One of the calls came from the

CEO of a hospital in the Bay Area, who had heard Dr. Patrascu speak at a presentation at the hospital. He said, "It sounds like Assist International is the door by which we can help Romania. We are upgrading our intensive care/critical care department and can donate our existing systems to you."

Bob said, "Yes, absolutely!" because he recalled a conversation he had had while in Romania with Dr. Vlaicu, a renowned cardiologist from Cluj who was a member of the New York Academy of Science. Dr. Vlaicu was a professor at the University of Cluj Medical Center and worked at the University Cardiology Hospital. He remembered that Dr. Vlaicu spoke of a need for heart monitors. It had hardly registered, as getting involved in medical equipment was the farthest thing from Bob's mind at the time. But Bob saw an opportunity and once again said yes, agreeing to take these monitors.

Bob called a member of his former church, who was a deputy with the Santa Cruz Police Department, and asked if he could help him pick up the cardiac care monitors from Bay Area hospital. They rented a U-Haul truck and picked up the monitors the next day. Through a series of connections, engineers from the manufacturer were able to join on the trip to Romania and install the cardiac care monitors at the University of Cluj Medical Center.

Something big and life-shaping was happening. What does it mean when we choose to embrace a challenge, at God's leading? One step leads on to another step, even though it's not clear at the time where we are going. As an example of this, another couple who heard about Assist International, George and Susan Schmidt, volunteered their commercial warehouse, along with packing shipments of equipment for many years in the early days of Assist International. As one writer says, "You can always find a reason to hesitate, to quit, or to delay jumping headfirst into your dreams, but you'll never step into the call on your life until you do."[28]

Bob and Char embraced the challenge before them. The two "Yes" answers Bob had given to help desperate needs in Romania—one Yes to Doctor Patrascu agreeing to itinerate him in the USA; followed by another Yes to accept cardiac care monitors that would ultimately go on to shape a global direction for Assist International that neither Bob nor Char could have imagined at the time.

CHAPTER FIVE

TAKING RISKS

Why not go out on a limb? That's where the fruit is.

—Frank Scully[29]

There will always be people who say that taking a risk is too great, no matter how enticing the possibility of reward. And there is some truth to it. Risk, just for the sake of the adrenaline rush, is simply not worth it for most of us. Bob and Char Pagett would agree with that. Nonetheless, they have taken plenty of risks in their lives.

Most of us would never even contemplate the risk Alex Honnold took. If you enjoy a handwringing, sweat-drenching adrenaline rush, watch the documentary *Free Solo*. It tells the story of Alex Honnold, the only person who successfully climbed the 2,900-foot face of El Capitan, a cliff of solid granite in Yosemite National Park, without using safety ropes. The path he chose was a zigzagging odyssey that traced several spidery networks of cracks and fissures, some gaping, others barely a knuckle wide. Along the way, Honnold squeezed his body into narrow chimneys, tiptoed across ledges the width of a matchbox, and in some places, dangled in the open air by his fingertips. And he did this *without any safety ropes, without a parachute, or any other protection.* If he had slipped even once, he would have fallen thousands of feet to his death.

In practicing for this climb with safety ropes, there was one difficult spot on the rock face where he was required to let go of his handhold and foothold and take a leap to another crevice in the rock. Several times as he attempted it with safety ropes, he slipped but was caught by his safety harness. Now, on this climb without any safety ropes, when he got to this place, he turned and waved to the camera crew below, knowing that in a few seconds, he would either be successful or cascade to his death. One of his cameramen, while leaving his camera focused on Alex, turned away. He later said, "I could not bear to watch, if Alex fell."

In November 2014, Clif Bar (the nutritional protein bar), which was a rock-climbing sponsor, announced that they would no longer sponsor Honnold, along with four other free solo climbers. "We concluded that this form of the sport is pushing boundaries and taking the element of risk to a place where we as a company are no longer willing to go," the company wrote in an open letter. This was at a time when some free solo rock climbers had already fallen to their death.

Bob, being a lover of the adrenaline rush all his life, purchased this movie and loved every minute. Char, on the other hand, hid her eyes and told Bob, "Get that movie out of the house; I never want to watch it again!"

Willing to Risk

When I (Bill) was twelve years old, our family had recently moved to Colorado and my sister Char was dating Bob. I recall Bob being competitive in just about everything. At age sixteen, Bob had purchased his own car, a 1947 Chevy. One of his best friends, Gordon, also owned his first car, a 1948 Ford. Of course, both Bob and Gordon had a friendly argument about who owned the fastest car.

On one occasion, I was riding with Gordon and some other kids to a church youth rally in another town, and my sister was riding with Bob and some other kids, both cars following each other on a winding two-lane highway. Bob was behind Gordon and decided to pass him. Both sped up, Gordon to avoid being passed and Bob flooring it to get around him. Bob barely made the pass before reaching a sharp curve; then Gordon, just as we reached a double yellow blind curve, swerved out to pass Bob. Char says she was yelling at Bob to slow down so Gordon could pass. For what seemed like several minutes and around a couple of blind curves, it was neck and neck. By then, I too was praying one of these "idiots" would concede. Char was now screaming at Bob, fearing her little brother (me) was about to be killed in a head-on collision. Finally, Bob conceded and let Gordon pass. I think if my parents had been told about this, maybe Bob would have never been given Char's hand in marriage. . . we just will never know. My sister, once her anger at Bob wore off, swore me to secrecy.

These stories illustrate how God, in his wisdom, put Bob and Char together to balance their life calling. Bob being a risk-taker and Char tending to be cautious helped bring balance in making wise and calculated risks that have often led to success in their humanitarian work.

Risks Worth Taking

A vision without a task is a dream; a task without a vision is drudgery; a vision and a task together are the hope of the world.

—from a church in Sussex, England, c. 1730

We all take risks every day. We risk driving our car to work. We risk our hearts when we agree to marriage. We take financial risks, such a buying a house or starting a company.

And some risks aren't worth putting our lives on the line. But a foolish risk is different from taking a calculated risk that is associated with our commitment of faith, to do what we feel God has called us to do. It is the object of our risk that matters. Faith is the ultimate risk. An unknown author wrote, "Upon a life I did not live; upon a death I did not die. Upon another's death, another's life—I risk my soul eternally."

We take risks when we step out to live our God-given purpose in life, whatever that may be. We take risks of faith because we know there is a grander plan that God has for people, and we want to be part of it. James Hudson Taylor, the legendary nineteenth-century missionary to China, once said, "Unless there is the element of extreme risk in our exploits for God, there is no need for faith."

Big Moments Call for Big Faith in a Big God

Since we have such a hope, we are very bold.
(2 Cor. 3:12)

Faith has a unique characteristic. It must be exercised to grow. We apply the faith—the confidence that we are doing God's work—to the challenge we are addressing. Are we afraid? Yes, at times. Do we always see the clear picture? Not always, and maybe never on this earth. But if the task we are attempting truly seems to be God's work, we step out and risk offering what we can offer to help others. Faith can produce amazing results.

To Russia with Love and Risk (Again)

In 1991, Doug Ross, a leader of Christian publishers, had by now become a good friend of Bob and Char's and asked if they would be willing to come to the second World's Book Fair in Moscow in September to help run the booth. Without hesitation, they agreed to participate.

Following the 1989 World's Book Fair in Moscow, the American Bible Society and the Evangelical Christian Publishers leadership had met with the mayor and city officials of Moscow and all the arrangements had been made—which included not only the distribution of four million more Bibles in the Russian language, but to hold a series of concerts at places like Gorky Park and, for the first time ever, in the Supreme Soviet building inside the Kremlin walls itself.

It was a time of immense political change inside the Soviet Union. Under Gorbachev, *perestroika* (a political movement for restoration) and *glasnost* (meaning openness) was having an effect. The old Soviet Union was coming apart, and many of the satellite countries such as Estonia, Latvia, Lithuania, Armenia, and Georgia had already declared their independence. The Berlin Wall had come down. Things in Russia seemed to be turning toward a more democratic and free society.

However, there was political trouble developing in Russia in the summer of 1991. Soviet hardliners and the KGB were not accepting the changes in *glasnost*. "A crisis spread across the Soviet Union nearing the time we were to leave for the Soviet Union for the World's Book Fair," Bob said, "No one knew for sure how this was going to play out. There could be civil war in Russia."

Gorbachev had gone to his *dacha* by the Black Sea, and word got out that he had been detained by hard-liner former KGB leaders to force a coup in Russia. This was the biggest crisis since

1917 in Russia. Nobody could predict what would become of the country, and nobody could predict whether this would begin a revolution that could sweep throughout Russia.

While this was taking place, Bob and Char were in the States, traveling by car toward their home and listening to news on the radio. Most of the news centered on the events taking place in Russia. There was an announcement that a coup attempt had taken place and that Mikhail Gorbachev was under house arrest. The Pagetts' daughters, Michelle and Cheri, called their parents, begging them to cancel their plans to go to Moscow.

When Bob and Char arrived home, they received a notice from the State Department warning them about travel to the Soviet Union and asking all American citizens to cancel their plans until they could see what the future would be in Russia.

Bob and Char thought and prayed, wondering what to do. A decision had to be made soon. Yes, there seemed to be potential danger in Russia. What would happen if a revolution took place and bullets were flying everywhere as they landed in Moscow? But there had been danger on the trip they'd recently completed in other parts of Eastern Europe. Both Bob and Char felt if ever there was a need for the events planned for Moscow to take place, it was now. They knew that four million Bibles had already been shipped to Moscow under the auspices of the Moscow Project, a joint effort with the Evangelical Christian Publishers, the International Bible Society, Youth for Christ International, and others. If the publishers did not come, who would help in the distribution of all these Bibles? Would the Bibles just be shredded by a new communistic regime?

When people of Christian faith like Bob and Char face a crisis, they usually turn to the Bible for guidance. This, of course, is what they did. As James 4:14–15 (TLB) declares, "How do you know what is going to happen tomorrow? For the length of your lives is as uncertain as the morning fog—now you see it; soon it is gone. What you ought to say is, 'If the Lord wants us to, we shall live and do this or that.'"

As they discussed what to do next, Bob and Char recalled how God had led them this far, as they went to Moscow the first time, then trusted God in leading them to resign their church, then witnessed the incredible changes in Romania and other parts of Eastern Europe. Would it be right to stop having faith in God's plan now? It did not seem right at this point to hold back. Moving forward now was in every fiber of Bob and Char's beings. They had a strong sense that they were following a path that God had put before them. They felt this calculated risk was worth it and they made the decision to continue their plans to go to Moscow.

John Piper said, "You can't put enough padlocks on your door and enough bars on your windows to keep a heart attack from happening. . . . There is no safety when traveling to get somewhere. There is no safety in the building while you are there. There are no guarantees that you are going to live another day. That is what experience teaches us. . . . There is no guarantee that anybody is going to take another breath. In terms of absolute security, all the efforts that we make to keep ourselves safe are ultimately an illusion."[30]

Fortunately, a short time before they were to depart, the coup against Gorbachev was aborted. Boris Yeltsin, then mayor of Moscow, stood on top of a tank and rallied the masses for President Gorbachev. The hardliners were imprisoned, and Gorbachev arrived back at the Kremlin in Moscow just two days before Bob and Char arrived in the country.

Only God could have known how this would play out, and Bob and Char's faith in knowing they were committed into His hands caused them to make a decision they would not regret.

When they arrived, the whole city seemed to be throbbing with joy. Bob and Char watched in amazement as the hammer-and-sickle flag was taken down and, in its place, the Russian Federation flag rose to the cheers of people. They were there when Gorbachev shut down the communist national headquarters office building and boarded it up. They saw the barricades that students and people had set up to keep the army at bay during the attempted coup. They saw the wreaths and the fresh blood on the streets where three young Soviet men had been run over by tanks. It was obviously a sacred place, as there were memorials, flowers, and candles, while people gathered and prayed. Someone had painted on a wall, "Forgive them, for they knew not what they were doing." Flowers were thrown on top of the military tanks, and people milled about with a sense of awe and wonder at what was happening.

To be an American at that time in Moscow was surreal, as the people loved seeing Americans. People warmly welcomed Bob and Char, throwing their arms around them, doing whatever they could to help them get around the city.

Unfortunately, the World's Book Fair had been cancelled due to the coup attempt. Originally many publishers committed to come to the book fair, but due to the perceived danger only a handful came, plus Bob and Char.

Undeterred, they went ahead with others from the Moscow Project, helping to distribute the Bibles in the streets and squares of Moscow. Russian soldiers helped them unload the boxes. They spread out everywhere with boxes of Bibles, giving them to anyone who asked for one, even though the book fair had been cancelled.

Char recalls being in an open-air market, giving Bibles to ladies who were selling flowers. "I turned around and started down the street in another direction and some of the ladies chased me down because they wanted a Bible," she said. "I gave Bibles to the soldiers, college students, merchants, and anyone who wanted one," Bob added. There seemed to be an insatiable hunger for the Bible, and four million copies of the Russian New Testament did not seem to be too many.

Despite the political chaos and uncertainty, the people with Youth for Christ International and the American Bible Society, along with Bob and Char representing the Christian publishers, proceeded with their plans for the concert in Gorky Park and for a concert at the Supreme Soviet building within the Kremlin walls.

On the day that the concert was to take place at the Supreme Soviet building inside the Kremlin walls, Bob and Char were on a bus allowed inside the Kremlin walls. The bus was loaded with the musical instruments and costumes of the ones who would be performing at the concert, along with six thousand Bibles that were to be given away to the six thousand Muscovites who had tickets to attend the event.

The evening before the concert, Bob and Char had attended a sumptuous dinner in the huge banquet hall on the top floor of the spectacular marble Supreme Soviet concert hall building where the concert would later be held. This was the historic hall where Gorbachev, Brezhnev, and Stalin had wined and dined the elite of the communist world including Fidel Castro and Ceausescu of Romania. Now the spectacular banquet hall was preparing a banquet for the Evangelical Christian Publishers, Youth for Christ International and the American Bible Society.

The master of ceremonies for the event was Jim Groen, President of Youth for Christ International, who presented a Bible to the local official in charge of the Supreme Soviet Building. The official graciously accepted the Bible, acknowledged the changes that were coming to his country, and said this was one of the most important gifts that he had ever received. He also said, "I have a thousand employees and if you could, I would like to provide a Bible for each of my employees."

That night the entertainment included several American musicians, and Larnelle Harris led everyone in singing, "Let us break bread together on our knees." Bob said, "Singing together in that banquet hall was one of the most riveting, historic moments we had ever experienced."

The same people who were on the streets just a few days earlier, hoping for some glimmer of hope for democracy and some change from the communist past, now were inside, many of them for the first time in an atmosphere where Christ was honored inside the Kremlin walls. Bibles were given to each of the people at the concert.

"The irony of that moment boggles my mind," Bob said. "The living Christ was being exalted within the Kremlin walls. We will be forever grateful that we took the risk and went ahead with that trip to Moscow. Only God knows how many lives were impacted by the events this opportunity provided," Bob said.

Now looking back nearly thirty years later at that dramatic moment in time for the rapidly changing Soviet Union and Bob and Char's involvement with helping to distribute Bibles, one must wonder at God's plan. Many in the West were hoping that Russia would be making important steps to a full democracy. But even more than the changes in the political system, four million copies of the Bible in the contemporary Russian language were given away. Governments rise and governments fall. The freedoms that looked to be emerging with such joy at that time in Russia seem to have now been dampened. And yet, opportunity was met through taking a risk. It was a unique moment in time that presented a unique opportunity that will bear fruit in years to come.

Scripture reminds us of God's words through the prophet Isaiah: "My thoughts are not your thoughts, nor are your ways My ways. . . . as the rain comes down, and the snow from heaven do not return there, but water the earth and make it bring forth and bud that it may give seed to the sower and bread to the eater. . . . So shall My word be that goes forth from My mouth; It shall not return to Me void, But it shall accomplish what I please, and it shall prosper in the thing for which I sent it" (Isa. 55:8, 20, 11, NKJV).

There is no way of knowing how many lives were changed in what was the Soviet Union at that time. We trust that the hope that was rekindled in many people burns still. The life of faith does not ask us to organize and strategize results. That, we leave up to God. We step out in obedience. We offer the cup of cold water. We meet the simplest needs. We give life-changing Scripture, and that is enough.

Why Take Risks?

There are three stages in the work of God: Impossible;
Difficult; Done.

—James H. Taylor

Accomplishing something significant often requires risk, and it requires stepping out of one's comfort zone. It requires faith.

There are humanitarian workers all over the world who work alongside dedicated local health-care workers who take incredible risks—doctors and nurses in every country who risk their own health to treat disease and viruses. First responders run into risk every day as they help others during natural disasters such as earthquakes, hurricanes, fires, and tsunamis, assisting people caught in the disaster. There are countless unsung heroes who give their lives to help the world's most vulnerable.

Bob and Charlene would be the first to admit that many times over the past thirty years they felt like they were "in over their heads" on some projects and ventures they had agreed to do. Dangerous close calls and project failures have, on occasion, happened. Sometimes the risks we take—even for all the right reasons—don't produce the results that we'd hoped for.

Bob described an incident that happened in Haiti. On January 12, 2010, a devastating 7.0 earthquake struck Haiti. The epicenter was near the town of Leogane. At least 200,000 people were killed, 300,000 injured, and thousands of buildings destroyed. Haiti is one of the poorest countries in the world and Assist International wanted to help. They sent a team along with a large shipment of food, medicine, bottled water, and other supplies.

Long-term, Assist hoped to also build an orphanage modeled after the successes they had in Romania and other parts of the world. But because of corruption in Haiti, it was difficult to know who was credible when trying to do business. Even on this first trip to Haiti right after the earthquake, members of the Assist team were threatened because they were giving out free bottles of purified water, and some locals were upset as it slowed their selling of water—water they had allegedly stolen from supplies sent in by USAID, which were supposed to be given away free.

On a second trip to Haiti, a delegation from Assist International had negotiated what they thought was a credible partner organization to purchase a ten-acre parcel of land. With the help of the local partners, they found a piece of land that supposedly belonged to one of the elected officials of the town, on which they would be able to build ten orphan family homes along with several new business ventures that would sustain the orphanage.

They met with the elected official. He said he believed in what Assist International wanted to do and offered the land. The official records of title were destroyed in the earthquake, but the local mayor was recognized as the proper owner of the property. A contract of terms was drawn up for the purchase of the land. What the A.I. team did not know was that another local person would soon also claim ownership of the land. The basis of the dispute stemmed from the fact that the original owner had abandoned the property and the official had declared eminent domain. As the records were lost in the earthquake, this gave opportunity for others to contend by force to assert ownership. The adjacent parcel had also been in contention, leading to three different claimants in dramatic confrontation, with guns drawn. In that moment all contending parties backed away, evacuating the property. Then similar tactics were used in an attempt to intimidate the humanitarian team.

Faced with this level of local lawlessness, continuing to push the issue was a greater risk than what Assist International was willing to take. Sadly, within one year following this horrible earthquake, many humanitarian efforts had ceased due to the corruption that was rampant in Haiti.

The incident in Haiti is just the tip of the iceberg in some of the inherent risks that team members of Assist International have faced.

Jim Stunkel, vice president of Assist International, recalled his first volunteer trip with Assist International, when he was invited by Tim Reynolds to ensure the delivery of supplies to an orphanage in Romania. Tim asked, "Do you want to join me and 'ride shotgun' on a shipment to Romania?"

Jim asked, "Do you mean 'ride shotgun,' like on a classic stagecoach of the old west? And by the way, isn't the guy who 'rides shotgun' the first one to be shot when the stagecoach is robbed?"

"Oh no, no problem," Tim said. "We will just be following the shipment to be sure it arrives securely."

Jim remembers thinking, *No problem! What could go wrong? Joining a friend for a good cause? Of course I would go.* Jim later recalled:

"We knew exactly what was in the shipment because we loaded the shipment ourselves. But when we arrived at the orphanage, only a fraction had been delivered. We immediately went to the warehouse of the transport company and found the supplies. The warehouse manager was a thief who did not anticipate we would be following the shipment. He also did not want to be exposed as a thief, so when we told him we would return with trucks and take the goods he did not try to stop us. The drama ended quickly, the supplies were recovered, orphan children were saved, and I could not wait to travel with Tim again.

"The next trips would not be disappointing. I joined Tim on a trip to Afghanistan in March of 2002, to make a needs assessment of two hospitals and an orphanage in Kabul. A doctor serving with the UN mission to Kabul was to be our point of contact, but we had no other information about how to make the connection. For more than a week before departing I called the office of the president of the San Francisco area Afghan Coalition to learn how to prepare for our program in Kabul. No one ever returned my calls.

"For travel plans, our airline booking ended in Pakistan because Afghanistan was not open to commercial air travel due to the war with the Taliban. But we presented ourselves and official documents regarding our program to the UN office in Islamabad and we were granted passage on a UN plane to Kabul for the following day. A bit of a relief because the alternative would have been to rent a car and drive over the Khyber Pass. Possible, but less safe.

"With a free afternoon we stopped in at a local hotel for a cup of tea, watching for anyone that may appear to be 'international,' possibly speak English, and be able to provide insight about how to find our way around once we arrive at Kabul. We met a man passing by that said he would also be on the UN plane, so we agreed to look for him the next day. The day passed, we met no one else, so we took dinner in the hotel. As we finished, we could hear women talking at a table behind us, and clearly their English accent sounded like home. We introduced ourselves and asked where they were from? San Francisco, San Jose, Palo Alto. What a coincidence. I asked them what brought them to Pakistan. One spoke up, 'We actually are heading home from Afghanistan, where we have been on a project because we are with the (San Francisco area) Afghan Coalition, I happen to be the president.'

"I took a very long breath. The president of the Afghan Coalition was exactly the person I had tried to contact, but failed to reach, for a week before we left. Although I had never met her before and would never have recognized her, yet now in a *seemingly* random encounter in Islamabad Pakistan, where I had never been before in my life, we just happened to choose the same hotel and restaurant, and just happened to sit at adjoining tables. I could not imagine the statistical probability of such an encounter happening by chance. But, by faith, I believe there are actual profound, divine appointments, and I certainly believe this was one of them. We were right where we were supposed to be.

"I told her that I had been trying to contact her to inquire about Kabul but was never able to get through, obviously because she had been in Afghanistan.

"She asked, 'Do you have a driver to take you around the city? What are your plans?'

"I told her we only had the names of the hospitals and a doctor to meet for the assessments, and my plan had been to meet her. She laughed and said, 'I do not expect you speak Farsi or Pashtun, and you will need a driver and translator.'

"After a thoughtful moment she said, 'Here is what you must do. Find Chicken Street. I do not know how you will, but it is famous, and you must find it, and once on Chicken find the Golden Finger jewelry store. Go in and ask for Ahmed; he speaks English. Tell him you need a driver and a translator, and he can hook you up.'

"Chicken Street, Golden Finger, Ahmed. We had a plan. The next morning at the UN plane we spotted the man we had met the prior day. We told him our plan and he said Chicken Street was near his home, although he happened to be from Italy, he explained he was working as a contractor in Kabul—for the very UN doctor we were looking for. Another divine appointment it would seem."

Jim added, "We made several more trips to Afghanistan in the following years, at times literally maneuvering through mine fields. Our work may lead to seemingly risky environments, but I am fully convinced if we are right where God wants us to be, we are in the safest place possible."

Bob also tells how God protected him from LRA rebels in South Sudan. The far northern part of Uganda and neighboring South Sudan is a dangerous place. This is where the LRA army operated from, kidnapping hundreds of children, murdering their parents, torturing, and killing thousands. It is the area where Sister Rosemary does her brave work (more about Sister Rosemary in chapter 9). It was Sister Rosemary's dream to replicate the work she was doing in Atiak, Uganda, at a remote village called Torit, located in South Sudan. Bob was in Juba City, South Sudan at the time, investigating if they should equip the critical care department of the hospital there to serve the people of South Sudan. Bob describes the trip:

"Without knowing anything about Torit, I agreed to join Sister Rosemary on a trip there. I got in the vehicle that they leased, along with their driver, joining Sister Rosemary and two other nuns to go to Torit. We started on a nice highway for a few miles, and then it turned onto a dirt road that led to Torit. It was one of the most dusty, bumpy roads I have ever been on, and it seemed to take forever to get there.

"On the way, there were some trucks blocking the road that appeared to have had an accident or breakdown. I found out later that some trucks would block the dirt road, where the drivers, by gunpoint, would take away the purses and wallets of the people behind them.

"Thankfully, we were able to proceed through the blockage. I found out later that it was probably because of the three nuns in our vehicle that they allowed us to pass. Once we arrived, we met city officials who showed us around including seeing some land that they were willing to donate if we would build an orphan village and a school.

"On our return trip, about halfway along the dusty, bumpy road, we ran out of gas. Our driver had forgotten to fill up with fuel before leaving. Here we were, in the middle of a jungle, on a bumpy dirt road, miles from nowhere, out of gas.

"We did not know what to do, so we prayed God would provide. After sitting there for about an hour, a truck came by, and I waved him down. I noticed on the side of the truck was a five-gallon can of fuel. After some negotiation, I was able to buy the gas in his can, and we made it back to Juba.

"That night, I had a scheduled meeting with the Minister of Health and the Minister of Security for South Sudan. I sat by the

Minister of Security for South Sudan. He asked where we had come from. I said, 'We just came back from Torit.' He looked shocked. He said, 'Torit? That is the most dangerous territory in South Sudan. Last week the rebels murdered the mayor of the city. There's a ruthless army hiding out in the jungle who are trying to overthrow the country. If they had met you, you would likely have been killed.'

"I had no idea that we had risked our lives to travel to Torit. But I know God knew. I also believe God protected us from meeting up with the rebels. It was another miracle how God protected us."

There is never an act of faith without risk. The apostle Paul was a risk-taker. In his second letter to the Corinthian church he said,

> I have worked harder, been put in jail more often, been whipped times without number, and faced death again and again and again. Five different times the Jews gave me their terrible thirty-nine lashes. Three times I was beaten with rods. Once I was stoned. Three times I was shipwrecked. Once I was in the open sea all night and the whole next day. I have traveled many weary miles and have been often in great danger from flooded rivers and from robbers and from my own people, the Jews, as well as from the hands of the Gentiles. I have faced grave dangers from mobs in the cities and from death in the deserts and in the stormy seas and from men who claim to be brothers in Christ but are not. I have lived with weariness and pain and sleepless nights. Often, I have been hungry and thirsty and have gone without food; often I have shivered with cold, without enough clothing to keep me warm. (1 Cor. 23–27, NLT)

Nancie and I went with Bob and Char on a "footsteps of Paul" trip a few years ago. One of the most moving experiences was a tour of the ruins of Ephesus. The coliseum was still there, where people had been entertained by prisoners fighting beasts, and usually being killed by the lions. I walked under the coliseum where the beasts came out of their den and where a prisoner would step out in the huge arena to fight them. Paul was imprisoned there, and he relates that he "fought wild beasts at Ephesus" (1 Cor. 15:32). Paul continued to risk his life to share the gospel, finally giving his life for this cause.

Jesus was also a risk-taker. He not only risked (and gave) His life for the redemption of the world, but He also risked using ordinary men and women to establish His church here on earth with His message of redemption to all. And through God's power and vision, ordinary people change the world.

Many others, like Bob and Char, are still working to change the world, still trying to carry out His mission of love and compassion to the least of these—no matter the risk.

Your "risk" may be quite different. Maybe it's just stepping out to give of your limited resources. Maybe it's becoming a foster parent to a child in need. Maybe it's taking your talents to another country to help with a short-term missions project. Maybe, like Bob and Char, it means quitting your current job to venture out into something new that you feel God is calling you to do. Risks like these are good risks, calculated risks that allow you to step out of your comfort zone and do something good for others that stretches your faith.

Great things rarely come from comfort zones!

CHAPTER SIX

SAYING YES TO THE OPPORTUNITY

There is hope in dreams, imagination, and in the courage of those who wish to make those dreams a reality.

—Jonas Salk[31]

Ray Schmidt was a key person to the success of Assist International in its early years. In fact, both Bob and Charlene give credit to Ray for his untiring work and feel that without Ray, the organization would not have grown into what it is today. Ray was an early hire at Assist who at first was operations coordinator and later executive vice president.

Ray said about Bob Pagett, "The biggest challenge for me at Assist International in my first few years was Bob's belief that nothing was impossible. He would say yes to almost everything. At that point we were still a small organization, which meant that many of the details and much of the planning fell to me. There were many times I wondered, 'What was Bob thinking?' But I learned something important in those early years: *nothing is impossible.* I will always be grateful to Bob for teaching me this powerful lesson that has stayed with me."

Bob believes that if a challenge is presented and it fits your mission, even if you are not sure yet where the resources are coming from or what might be needed to complete the project, go ahead and say Yes—and then figure out how to get the job done.

Saying Yes is not as simple as it sounds and can have many layers. And while the Assist International staff has embraced the concept of accepting impossible challenges to meet a need, they now frame it as a "value-added service."

Consequently, Bob's tendency to say yes to needs has widened into a value-added principle and philosophy Assist International uses to this day, as many individuals within Assist International are willing to tackle just about anything to help those in need.

Figuring Out the Yes

It's not that I'm so smart, it's just that I stay with problems longer.

—Albert Einstein[32]

The principle of saying Yes to opportunities that fit your mission before you have all the logistics and people in place may appear to be an unlikely guiding principle. But saying Yes to meeting a need is a powerful first step. It is an act of faith, believing God will provide the rest of the pieces to meet the need.

Saying Yes is also a willingness to try. It involves faith, yes, but also hard work, persistence, creativity, and innovation. Thomas Edison once said, "Most people miss opportunity because it is dressed in overalls and looks like work."

An example of this is what Tim Reynolds was able to accomplish while building new orphanage homes in Romania. Tim, a licensed building contractor and vice president of Assist International's on-site development teams, was another key employee in those early days. Shortly after the fall of communism in Romania, there was a shortage of both building supplies and skilled professionals to accomplish the task of building orphanage homes in Romania. Tim devised a plan whereby the lumber needed was all precut prior to shipping; and all the needed materials such as electrical, plumbing, sheetrock, etc., were then loaded into forty-foot containers and shipped to Romania. Then, Tim took groups of volunteer professionals to Romania, where they were able to assemble and complete the construction of these homes in a matter of days, usually in less than two weeks.

Since Assist International works in many countries and villages of the world where the infrastructure is limited it may require building all or part of the infrastructure before the primary goal can be accomplished. It has and continues to be the mandate of Assist International to work with in-country partners to design projects and programs that fit their needs and local context.

Later, Tim transitioned from building orphan homes in Romania to building hospital facilities in Africa. For example, the goal may be to bring in a cardiac care system to a hospital in a remote location. An entire intensive care unit or surgical theater for a hospital, with all the supportive infrastructure utilities, may be needed. Then, once the room is built, the electrical system is working, and the water is being filtered, a biomed team can come in and install the monitors or surgical equipment—followed by doctors, biomed engineers, and nurses who can train local doctors and staff how to use whatever equipment has been installed. One thing calls for another.

"We began to look for ways to bring added value to our partners in creative ways," Tim said. "We started with power generators and that led to water filtration systems. Soon we were doing 66,000-cubic-meter water tanks that were constructed nine meters up in the air. We became the trusted eyes, ears, and doers on the ground for our organizational partners."

If a building needs to be constructed, Assist International is now positioned to say, "We have skilled and qualified people and partners who can work alongside the local workforce and build that." If a clean water filtration system or a new electrical generation system is needed, Assist International can get it done in a fast and cost-effective way. Today, Assist International plays a major role in addressing the need of "access to medical oxygen." Having built PSA plants in several global south countries in partnership with a major corporate foundation, the COVID-19 pandemic has made access to medical oxygen one of the major priorities; patients need medical oxygen to survive. If there is a need for clinical or technical training for health care professionals and technicians, Assist International has a pool of professionals to draw from to bring the needed training. If another orphan home needs to be built at one of the orphan villages they sponsor, Assist International has networked to link skilled international engineers and builders to partner with in-country skilled labor to complete projects at the highest standards.

From the beginning of Assist International, Bob sought out and brought licensed people in their field of expertise to help with the projects. Because of Bob's willingness and capacity to network and recruit a team of experts, Assist International can now provide a large array of value-added services to their partners. Doctors, nurses, biomed engineers, skilled construction workers of all trades see the opportunity to take a trip overseas to help build capacity alongside their in-country partners to meet important needs. They recognize that their training and work can be applied to provide meaningful support to make a difference in the lives of others.

Saying an all-encompassing Yes to get a needed project done is an important principle that Assist International has adopted that has made a huge difference in attracting major partnerships and donors to work with them.

"Yes" Can Mean Bumps in the Road

When the world says give up,
Hope says try one more time.

—Unknown

While it is no doubt true that Bob "flew by the seat of his pants" in the beginning stages of Assist International, make no mistake that he was highly skilled at finding ways to fulfill his promise and recruit highly skilled professionals to work directly with the local officials. And, as Assist International progressed, Bob and Char and their staff quickly learned from their experience, which consequently raised the standards of how to complete international projects in the global south by training and equipping in-country partners and the local workforce.

Of course, this was several years after Assist International had started. There were several painful lessons learned to get to this point. Obviously, it is impossible to meet every need put before us. We cannot say Yes to everything. But being aware of a critical need of desperate people—and the knowledge that maybe, just maybe, you can help meet that need. . . you can connect with someone who can provide that medical help. . .

or that there's a way to provide safety for orphaned and sick children—these possibilities have compelled Bob and Char and their team to at least try. To say Yes. Char freely admits, "We were driven."

All things are possible to him who believes, yet more to him who hopes; more still to him who loves; and most of all to him who practices these three virtues.

—Brother Lawrence

Getting It Done

In an earlier chapter, we described the first medical project that Bob and Char did in the fall of 1991, which was to install cardiac care monitors at the University of Cluj Medical Center in Romania. But before these monitors were ready to ship, it was decided that in addition to installing the heart monitors in Cluj they would also take some dialysis machines to a dialysis clinic in Bucharest.

Bob asked Paul Lynch, a respiration therapist and member of Bob's former church, to help him find a team to install the equipment. Paul introduced Bob to Brad Carrott, who became a major participant in the biomed help that Assist International needed. For weeks, the team worked to prepare the equipment for shipping and prepare medical seminars and seminar notes translated into the Romanian language.

Finally, all the equipment was bubble-wrapped, put into freshly built wooden containers, and shipped to Romania. Bay Area news teams had done stories to document what was happening, and interest in Assist International continued to increase. The team was excited to be going on their very first medical mission to Romania.

When the team arrived with Bob in Bucharest, it was big news in Romania: an American team had arrived to do some wonderful work in the capital city of Bucharest. For the team, it was a stark experience. Hotels were run-down, they were cold and dark due to lack of heat, and every room had cockroaches. The team groped through dark hallways to find their rooms. Bob tells the story that one member of the team spilled some water on the floor, and within a couple of minutes it was frozen.

When the team arrived at the dialysis center the next morning, the crates were opened, and the dialysis machines were rolled to the center of the room along with various other accessories. Big moment! It was then that the director of the center said, "Is this all that you sent with these dialysis machines?"

"Yes," Bob said. "Is there something wrong?"

The director said, "The blood pumps are missing. Dialysis machines don't work without blood pumps."

Bob was embarrassed and heartsick. This was Assist International's very first medical project and the blood pumps, wrapped in bubble wrap, were still somewhere in the warehouse in California.

They boarded a train to go from Budapest to Cluj to install the cardiac care monitors. He and Char fretted the entire train trip about what they would find in the crates shipped to Cluj and if all the equipment and accessories would be there.

As it turned out, all the equipment and needed accessories were in the containers, and the project went perfectly. Everyone on the team, including Brad Carrott, worked hard to follow instructions, drill holes, and string wires to hook up the machines. The medical seminar and teaching went well, with the local medical staff soaking up the information and training. Dr. Vlaicu was thrilled with the project as it brought the hospital, which prior to this had been using 1950s technology, up to similar standards in cardiac monitoring that could be found in any well-developed country. It was a touching and emotional moment for everyone.

And three weeks later, the blood pumps were delivered to the dialysis center in Bucharest and the resident director was able to install and finish the project without the help of the team.

But complications and the stress of this trip caused Bob and Char to reconsider if they were doing the right thing in doing medical projects. Sometimes the stress and anxiety of whatever it is we are called to do can cause us to reconsider our mission. At that time in the early years of Assist International, Bob became hesitant about ever doing medical projects again. The embarrassment of the missing blood pumps stuck with him; and the stress in the Cluj project, while rewarding, was exhausting. On the plane trip home, Bob said to Char, "I think this is the last medical project we will ever do." Char agreed.

But while that was a "bump in the road," it was not to be their last medical project. God had other plans that, at the time, they could not foresee. Little did they realize that the biomed engineers who had been on the team with them to Romania were headed to the Association for the Advancement of Medical Instrumentation (AAMI) conference being held at the Disneyland Hotel. All the major medical equipment companies were in attendance. The biomed engineers who had been with Bob and Char were so excited about what they had done in Romania that they held an open forum about their trip; by the time the seminar ended, more than one hundred biomed engineers and other medical experts had signed up, wanting to volunteer on the next medical project Assist International might be doing.

While this was happening, and shortly after returning from Romania, Bob received a call from Dr. Huldah Buntain, director of Mission of Mercy Hospital in Calcutta, India. She had heard about Assist International in a rather roundabout way. She was speaking at a church in Sacramento and read a notice in the church bulletin about their church helping to sponsor a medical project with Assist International in Romania. "Bob, I desperately need a monitoring system for our critical care and intensive care units in my hospital," Huldah said. She went on to explain the plight of the people of Calcutta and the critical need for monitoring equipment because people were dying without having a way to monitor their basic vital signs. She also mentioned that the Mission of Mercy Hospital was the hospital that Mother Teresa used for herself and the people she ministered to. Of course, after a short pause, Bob said, "Okay Huldah, I'll see what we can do." Bob could not resist the plea for help, and so he answered with another Yes.

On Monday morning, Bob received a call from Dr. David Harrington, chief of biomedical engineering for New England Medical Center in Boston and one of the founding leaders of the Association for the Advancement of Medical Instrumentation. He had witnessed the enthusiasm of the team that was at the conference.

"I recently heard about Assist International and wanted to meet you and know more about the organization," he said. He shared that he had written articles in the *New England Medical Journal* on the dos and don'ts of bringing medical equipment to developing countries.

After doing some brief research, Bob discovered that David was a renowned biomed engineer, and a part of a team that designed the space suits for NASA's astronauts who landed on the moon. With some of David's technology, along with the team assigned to design the spacesuits, the astronauts were able to move away from the space capsule and walk on the moon.

Tuesday morning, Bob was on a plane headed to the John Wayne Airport in Anaheim, California. As he and David Harrington met over lunch, David asked, "What projects do you have coming up?" Bob said, "Last Saturday night I received a call from Dr. Huldah Buntain, director of Mission of Mercy Hospital in Calcutta. She is in desperate need of monitors for the critical care units of the hospital." Bob went on to share how Mother Teresa and her Sisters of Charity received their medical care at the hospital free of charge, and that the hospital also cared for the orphan children under Mother Teresa's care.

David responded, "I'm an Irish Catholic from Boston, and I want to be involved in this project in Calcutta."

Before long, a team of biomedical engineers put together by David Harrington joined Bob on a trip to Calcutta to do the medical project.

Meeting Mother Teresa

Tell me how much you know of the sufferings of your fellow man, and I will tell you how much you have loved them.

—Helmut Thielicke[33]

The magnitude of being with someone like Mother Teresa, even if only for a few hours, can profoundly change the course of one's life. The medical team was told that Mother Teresa had just returned from an overseas trip and wanted to meet them. On a Sunday evening the team was ushered into the convent. As they entered the room where they were to meet Mother Teresa, Bob noticed how stark yet immaculately clean the room was, with an uncarpeted cement floor and only a few rugs. The wooden furniture was sturdy but plain, and there was no air conditioning. They later learned that Mother Teresa had refused to live above the poor that God had called her to reach. In Bob's mind it was a huge sacrifice to not have air conditioning in hot, humid, and sticky Calcutta, an impoverished city with such pollution that in the early days some called it the "armpit of the world."

Mother Teresa entered the room in a simple linen gown that nearly reached the floor and wore sandals that showed her gnarled feet and twisted toes. She greeted each member of the team, giving each person her undivided attention, deeply interested in each person. She asked how the project was going. She shared her love for the Mission of Mercy Hospital and Dr. Huldah Buntain, and she was grateful the hospital was open to all under her care. Pictures were taken with each member with Mother Teresa before their farewells.

On Monday, the team worked feverishly on the project, hurrying to finish it. Late that afternoon, Huldah came to the ICU to check in on everyone to see how the installation was going. She also said that Mother Teresa wanted the team to come the next day so they could visit one of her orphanages and the hospice for the dying. The next day, the medical team journeyed to Mother Teresa's convent in a Mission of Mercy ambulance. When they arrived at the convent, nuns were passing out buckets of water from a water truck to a cistern in the convent compound. The Assist team immediately got out of the ambulance and started helping. Not certain as to whether Mother Teresa would join them or send a representative, they were suddenly thrilled when Mother Teresa walked out the door to lead them herself. She waved off her driver and vehicle and climbed into the ambulance being used for transportation, along with the rest of the team, and off they went through the heavy, congested, and polluted traffic of Calcutta.

There are no traffic rules in Calcutta. Side doors of most cars on the streets are scratched and dented. People folded their car-side mirrors because the cars would drive so close to each other that the mirrors would be torn off. Mother Teresa seemed oblivious to the congestion as she gave the team her undivided attention. The curtains of the ambulance were closed, and at one point the ambulance was stopped for about ten minutes with no traffic moving. Mother Teresa opened the curtain to look out to see what was happening. When the Indian traffic cop saw that it was her, he began to blow his whistle, ordering vehicles to either move to the left or right so that Mother Teresa could get through. One small car that was stalled on the street was lifted by a dozen Indians a few feet so the ambulance could get through. It reminded Bob of one of the Beatitudes, "The meek shall inherit the earth." This small, humble, unassuming, deeply spiritual woman, recognized the world over, was so respected by the people in Calcutta that they made sure she could get through the congested traffic to her destination. It was said that Mother Teresa did not need a passport to enter any country, and that no airline charged her airfare and usually seated her in first class.

At the hospice, there was an atmosphere of peace and serenity, with Bible verses and inspirational quotes on the walls. Volunteers gave critically ill people water, trying to make them as comfortable as possible. Mother Teresa went to each cot, laying her hands on each person, praying a simple but earnest prayer. Bob saw her go to a woman with leprosy that had eaten away at her face where she had no nose or lips; her face looked like a huge hole. Mother Teresa tenderly placed her hand over the women's disfigured face and prayed for her. Mother Teresa wrote, "Kind words can be short and easy to speak, but their echoes are truly endless." By her simple yet profoundly kind example, she has greatly impacted the world.

Upstairs was Mother Teresa's private place of prayer, with a sign at the bottom of the stairs that said, "No Entrance." But she said to the medical team, "Come with me." In the room was a kneeling bench with a picture of Jesus and Mary, the mother of Jesus. There were spiritual quotes on the walls and a sacred sense of the presence of God in the place. She spent a moment in prayer there, and then the team continued the tour.

They visited one of her orphanages in Calcutta where there were children in dire physical condition being cared for by respectful, loving nuns. Bob noticed a terribly disfigured little girl, as caring people were trying their best to feed her. Bob thought that her existence on this earth surely could not be long, but the nuns were making her as comfortable as possible.

When the project was finished at the hospital and the commissioning completed, one of the biomedical engineers, an elderly but strong man, privately told his story to Bob.

"I was an eighteen-year-old soldier in World War II. Our battalion was one that rescued the holocaust victims in Dachau. I saw the emaciated people left there, the open pits where the dead were dumped, and the gas ovens of death," he said. "Seeing this, I thought if there was a God, He would never allow something like this to happen and it was there that I lost my faith." He went on to say, "Here in Calcutta is the first time my heart has been open to God, and because of what I have experienced my faith has been restored."

The residual benefit of doing the work that Assist International does is to see what it can do in the hearts of those who volunteer to go on these projects. It has a way of not only changing their view of the world and their appreciation for their life, but it can often bring personal inner healing to them in ways that nothing else can. And the trip to Calcutta also changed the trajectory of Assist International.

The Human Element of the Yes

Courage doesn't always roar. Sometimes courage is
the quiet voice at the end of the day saying, "I will try
again tomorrow."

—Mary Anne Radmacher[34]

As mentioned at the beginning of this book, medical projects, now numbering in the hundreds, have become a major part of what Assist International does. But even with lots of experience and a well-laid-out plan, not everything goes smoothly on every project. Many things can complicate the best-laid plans. Shipping delays, flight cancellations, customs glitches, team members getting sick, and other unforeseen issues can hamper any project.

But regardless of obstacles, we can press on to finish what we started—and work out the details after we have said Yes. One of Bob's strengths was that he simply would not take no for an answer. When an obstacle was placed before him, he just kept pushing, negotiating, and looking for a solution.

Everyone Can Say Yes

There are no shortages of crisis situations in most parts of the world. The coronavirus is an unprecedented example. Human suffering is massive and overwhelming on a world scale in this pandemic. There are problems everywhere to be solved. But we can never forget that there are also people, foundations, service organizations, and corporations who want to help. And it is because of this that, out of crisis, opportunity can arise.

The crisis may not be on a global scale. In fact, most likely there is someone in your neighborhood, your Rotary group, your family, or your church who is facing some sort of crisis: a recent

hai spoke excellent English. "Welcome to our home," he
Moving toward the kitchen he introduced us to his dark-
wife Nicoleta, who was fixing lunch for the children. She
her hand and a pleasant smile. Two large refrigerators
ied most of one wall in the kitchen, which was adjacent to a
lining area with tables to seat twenty.

s we walked down the long hallway, Mihai explained that
ome was designed to house sixteen children. Bedrooms were
ated into two sections, half of which were on one side for the
and the other half for the girls, with a master bedroom in the
lle for Mihai and Nicoleta.

Nancie and I were visiting the Caminul Felix Orphanages in
dea, Romania, as part of our research for this book. *Caminul*
x means "happy home." Caminul Felix One is a compound
le up of six homes, each staffed by parents who have up to
een children per home. In addition, there is an administrative
lding, some craft and other outbuildings, and a playground
the center which the homes surround in a semicircle. (Cami-
l Felix Two is in another area of Oradea, with ten homes and a
pporting village along with other buildings and a dairy farm.)

When the tour of Mihai and Nicoleta's house was finished,
e sat down in a small comfortable den next to the living area to
ten to Mihai's story of how it came to be that he and Nicoleta
ecame house parents.

"Nicoleta and I came to Caminul Felix right after our hon-
ymoon. It was not long after the revolution and we saw the
huge problem of orphaned kids in our country, which was the
hidden part of Romania before the revolution. We had read
about the Caminul Felix Orphanage and decided it would be
nice to see what they did. When we showed up, we saw homes
being built and saw the plan to have a parent couple in each

diagnosis of cancer, a death or accident in the family, the loss of
a job. Someone may be suffering from depression, a divorce, an
addiction, or some other crisis where you can simply offer your
presence—a listening ear, or a warm meal. Simple, spontaneous
things we do out of love and caring can become a profound
turning point in a person's life. In each life, there are small, but
profound "Mother Teresa moments" where we can offer hope and
kindness to those who are in need.

Our neighbor down the street recently lost her husband and
shortly thereafter we had a major snowstorm. Having a snow
blower, I plowed my own driveway and decided to go down and
plow her driveway. It was a quick and simple gesture on my part,
but I was surprised by the deep satisfaction I felt in doing it, which
was far more rewarding than the thirty minutes it took me to do
it. In fact, it felt so good that I ended up plowing the driveways of
three more of my neighbors. Small gestures of caring and kindness
right where we are can change someone's world.

Out of crisis and need comes opportunity. It might require a
new way of thinking and it will almost always require creativity
and innovation to accomplish what is needed.

CHAPTER SEVI

THE POWER OF O

I am only one, but still, I am on
I cannot do everything, but still, I can do
And because I cannot do everything, let m
To do something I can do.

—Edward Everett Hale[35]

"*This is not my job, it's my life!*"
The house was a simple one-story hom
painted siding and white shutters on the windows
shrub border lined the walkway to the front door, w
to the right that appeared to be a climbing rose bush.
girls sitting on a bench smiled as Nancie and I appr
were here to see firsthand the work at Caminul Felix i.
and wanted to meet some of the house parents.

Waiting at the front door was Mihai, a well-built n
early sixties with a broad smile. The father of this home s
hands and ushered us inside.

Mi
said. N
haired
offere
occup
large
A
the h
sepa
boys
mid

Ora
Feli
ma
six
bu
in
nu
su

w
li
b

diagnosis of cancer, a death or accident in the family, the loss of a job. Someone may be suffering from depression, a divorce, an addiction, or some other crisis where you can simply offer your presence—a listening ear, or a warm meal. Simple, spontaneous things we do out of love and caring can become a profound turning point in a person's life. In each life, there are small, but profound "Mother Teresa moments" where we can offer hope and kindness to those who are in need.

Our neighbor down the street recently lost her husband and shortly thereafter we had a major snowstorm. Having a snow blower, I plowed my own driveway and decided to go down and plow her driveway. It was a quick and simple gesture on my part, but I was surprised by the deep satisfaction I felt in doing it, which was far more rewarding than the thirty minutes it took me to do it. In fact, it felt so good that I ended up plowing the driveways of three more of my neighbors. Small gestures of caring and kindness right where we are can change someone's world.

Out of crisis and need comes opportunity. It might require a new way of thinking and it will almost always require creativity and innovation to accomplish what is needed.

CHAPTER SEVEN

THE POWER OF ONE

I am only one, but still, I am one.
I cannot do everything, but still, I can do something.
And because I cannot do everything, let me not refuse
To do something I can do.

—Edward Everett Hale[35]

"*This is not my job, it's my life!*"

The house was a simple one-story home with blue-painted siding and white shutters on the windows. A trimmed shrub border lined the walkway to the front door, with an arbor to the right that appeared to be a climbing rose bush. Two teenage girls sitting on a bench smiled as Nancie and I approached. We were here to see firsthand the work at Caminul Felix in Romania and wanted to meet some of the house parents.

Waiting at the front door was Mihai, a well-built man in his early sixties with a broad smile. The father of this home shook our hands and ushered us inside.

Mihai spoke excellent English. "Welcome to our home," he said. Moving toward the kitchen he introduced us to his dark-haired wife Nicoleta, who was fixing lunch for the children. She offered her hand and a pleasant smile. Two large refrigerators occupied most of one wall in the kitchen, which was adjacent to a large dining area with tables to seat twenty.

As we walked down the long hallway, Mihai explained that the home was designed to house sixteen children. Bedrooms were separated into two sections, half of which were on one side for the boys and the other half for the girls, with a master bedroom in the middle for Mihai and Nicoleta.

Nancie and I were visiting the Caminul Felix Orphanages in Oradea, Romania, as part of our research for this book. *Caminul Felix* means "happy home." Caminul Felix One is a compound made up of six homes, each staffed by parents who have up to sixteen children per home. In addition, there is an administrative building, some craft and other outbuildings, and a playground in the center which the homes surround in a semicircle. (Caminul Felix Two is in another area of Oradea, with ten homes and a supporting village along with other buildings and a dairy farm.)

When the tour of Mihai and Nicoleta's house was finished, we sat down in a small comfortable den next to the living area to listen to Mihai's story of how it came to be that he and Nicoleta became house parents.

"Nicoleta and I came to Caminul Felix right after our honeymoon. It was not long after the revolution and we saw the huge problem of orphaned kids in our country, which was the hidden part of Romania before the revolution. We had read about the Caminul Felix Orphanage and decided it would be nice to see what they did. When we showed up, we saw homes being built and saw the plan to have a parent couple in each home. Some homes were already finished and there were children playing in the yard."

Mihai continued, "As I walked the grounds, I was moved with compassion and the challenge that was facing my country and my city with so many orphans. I looked at Nicoleta and said, 'I think God wants us to be here.' She smiled and squeezed my hand as tears welled up in her eyes. We both just knew it was 100 percent God's will for us to be here."

At the time, Mihai was a recent college graduate with a degree in geology and had options for a good job. "We were young and had no children of our own at the time and knew nothing about parenting. But we knew we needed to apply for being house parents. The home we sit in now has been our home since we began twenty-seven years ago." Making a sweeping gesture toward the window where several children were sitting on benches in the yard, he proudly said, "These are all my children now."

He and Nicoleta continued to fill the beds of their home with orphaned children for twenty-seven years, as others grew up and moved out on their own. "We now have thirty-six children" (including two biological children), he smiled. "Seven of our children are married and we now have seven grandchildren!"

We asked him, "Mihai, why did you and Nicoleta give your entire adult lives to parenting orphans?"

He thought for a moment. Then tears came to his eyes. Pointing to a couple of his children who wandered past the living room in that moment, he said, "I am here because they are here!" He added passionately, "This is not my job; it is my life."

Before we left, Mihai said, "Now that Nicoleta and I are getting older, we cannot take the young orphans anymore. We have been parents now for almost thirty years. We have had many of our children since they were infants. If we took more, we worry we might die before they are fully raised. We have only five children left at home now, the youngest being eight. Some of our children will be leaving for college soon. I told the supervisor that I would like to move out to an apartment of my own with my five children so they can fill this house again. There are sixteen beds for children in this house. I hate looking at empty beds, so I want a young couple to take over this house so that once again, all beds will be filled with orphaned children who need a home."

We asked Mihai what their philosophy was for raising all these children from various backgrounds.

"Just love," he said. "It is not complicated. There is no formula, no philosophical narrative and no counseling that works like love to cure the mental and emotional damage my children may have suffered before coming here. God called Nicoleta and me to love and care for each one of them." He added, "God helps us every day. We could not survive without His mercy, His strength."

The Healing Power of Love

Never believe that a few caring people can't change the world. For indeed, that's all who ever have.

—Margaret Mead[36]

Cristiana's life was changed by the power of love when she was a young girl of eleven, burdened with caring for her little brothers as her parents struggled to survive under an oppressive communistic regime and their own family issues of alcoholism and domestic violence. She says, "I was too little to understand how things work in this world, but I wasn't too little to realize something wasn't right with my family." At her young age, Cristiana was forced to be the caretaker for her infant brother. "There were nights when I only slept for a few hours due to the care of my baby brother. And then I still needed to go to school the next day," she said.

Life became so hard that Cristiana and her siblings finally ended up with her grandparents. "But things went from bad to worse when my grandfather died," she said. "My grandmother simply had no way to care for us."

That is when Caminul Felix Orphanage found out about Cristiana and her siblings. "The thought of leaving home made me scared and joyful at the same time. I knew that with the situation my family was in at that point, my brothers and I would have no future. We left home hoping that things would be better, but I did not know exactly what that would mean. But from the moment I arrived at Caminul Felix until today, God has overwhelmed me with His gifts. I was impressed by the beautiful home I got to live in, by the fact that I had my own room and so many new things. Everything seemed too good to be true! Yet, the greatest blessing He had for me were the people who were going to be my parents. It was difficult to get used to that idea, but now, after all the years spent with them, when I think about 'mom and dad,' I see their image in my mind. They showed me what a family means. I felt loved and encouraged. They rejoiced for my successes, they were with me when I was sad and disappointed. They warned me and reproved me when I made mistakes."

After high school, Cristiana went to college, then on to medical school. Today, the little girl who was tormented by the fact that her little brother had nothing to eat is now a practicing pediatrician at the Cluj University Hospital. Cristiana, through her participation in the Caminul Felix Orphan Choir tours, visited places like the United States, England, Sweden, and Norway. "As a child, I had never dared to dream of such opportunities!" she exclaimed.

But love restored her and gave her a dream, as she now cares for children in her practice. Love begets love.

These stories come from homes that Assist International has been instrumental in helping to build and furnish. As inspiring as it is to see the actual buildings which Assist International has faithfully helped to build and support (which is vital for any of this work to exist), it's even more inspiring to hear the stories of how these homes have changed the lives of so many children. It brings purpose and life to realize these children have been given a future and a hope.

Love Sees the "One"

And whoever gives one of these little ones only a cup of cold water in the name of a disciple, assuredly, I say to you, he shall by no means lose his reward.

—Matt. 10:42, NKJV

When we see statistics of orphans and vulnerable people, millions of them living in refugee camps or cardboard shacks with open sewage, plus the devastation caused by war and famine and disease throughout the world, we can feel overwhelmed. Some of us are tempted to turn away, wondering what we can possibly do to help. We want to make a difference, but it seems too much. However, we *can* see the one.

Bob and Char have been driven by their life's work to see the "one"—each individual need. Perhaps it springs out of the unthinkable loss of their baby daughter Pammy to want to rescue the "one." They also see it as a moral and scriptural imperative. Bob said, "The Bible is filled with scriptures that give us a road map on how we should respond to the world's most vulnerable.

There are more than two thousand scriptures in the Old Testament alone dealing with God's concern for the poor. Two scriptures are important to us: 'Religion that God our Father accepts as pure and faultless is this: to look after orphans and widows in their distress and to keep oneself from being polluted by the world' (James 1:27). And the writer of Proverbs says, 'Speak up for those who cannot speak for themselves, for the rights of all who are destitute. Speak up and judge fairly; defend the rights of the poor and needy' (Prov. 31:8–9)."

The principle of seeing the "one" has turned into seeing and helping the many. But it always starts with one.

Caminul Felix Orphan Homes is sponsored by both Assist International and a group from Sweden. Lars Hornberg, founder of Caminul Felix, left Sweden for Romania to start the orphan homes. Bob and Char met Lars through meeting his late wife Linda, who was from the States; and when they heard the story of Caminul Felix from Linda, they wanted to be involved. Bob and Char simply began doing what they do when they find a viable work that is helping the most vulnerable. One thing they did early on became an incredible commitment, and it was an amazing miracle how it came together.

In 1995, Bob and Char agreed to try to fulfill a dream Lars and Linda had to bring the first Romania Orphan Choir to the United States to tour and raise support. They knew that if people here in the USA could see these precious children who have been rescued and given hope, it would inspire others.

But bringing a large group of orphan kids to the United States was not as simple as it might sound! The logistics of bringing thirty orphans to America as a choir is fraught with detailed issues. All of them needed visas, all of them needed airfare, all of them needed a way to get from place to place once they were here. Not to mention the scheduling of meetings for them in churches, schools, etc., and places for them to be housed and fed. Not many of us would tackle a monumental task like this.

First, Bob called the US Embassy to see about getting visas for the children. He was told that if they were orphans, they did not qualify for a visa due to US policy. The state department was already concerned about Romanians coming to the USA on visitor visas and then staying in the country. The last thing they wanted was a group of orphans coming in bunches to the USA, knowing the demand there to adopt children.

It should be noted here that the philosophy of Caminul Felix is to raise the children in their home country to be leaders there, instead of adopting them out to foreign countries. That continues to be a positive and affirming aspect of all the orphanages Assist International works with—building within the country instead of sending the children to other countries for adoption.

Bob explained to the consulate that an orphanage was being provided for these children and there were parents for them in the orphanage. Finally, Bob contacted Congressman Frank Wolfe, who was familiar with the work that Assist International was doing. Congressman Wolfe's letter convinced the authorities to grant the visas, on the conditions that round-trip airline tickets be purchased prior to the granting of the visas and that Assist International would take full responsibility for these children and guarantee the return of all of them to Romania.

Next, Bob called to book the airfares. The cost was going to be $38,000, which was money that Assist International did not have—so Bob told the airline agent he wanted to put it on his airline visa card. Since $38,000 was over his credit card limit, he had to call the bank that issued the credit card. Bob said, "The bank officer laughed and said, 'No way. . . you just want to get a lot of free miles!'" So Bob pulled out his rarely used American Express card that he received years ago when he was a youth minister, and that credit card company allowed him to book the flight. He held his breath and prayed a prayer as the card was processing. The card went through for the full amount and the tickets were purchased.

"I went to bed that night and began to worry. How could we possibly pay that American Express bill which would arrive before the choir would come and before any funds would be donated?" Bob said. "Finally, I just said, 'Lord, I trust you to somehow provide.'"

The next day, there was a knock on their door. A gentleman Bob had known for a short while, who had heard what Bob was trying to accomplish, was at the door. He handed Bob an envelope, saying it was a gift to help the choir come to America.

"We thanked him, thinking maybe it was $500 or $1,000," Char said, "After he left, we opened the envelope and in it was a check for $25,000. We were amazed and put that $25,000 on our next American Express bill." By the time the following month's bill came in, there was enough from the choir offerings to pay the balance.

Next was the problem of transportation across America once the choir arrived. Bob called Greyhound Bus Lines and they told him it would cost $60,000 to take the choir from New York across America on tour. "There was no way we could possibly afford that amount," Bob said.

Bob and Char's daughter Michelle remembered a friend from college who was working for a bus company. Bob contacted him to see if there was a bus available. He said they had a refurbished bus they would sell him for $18,000. That sounded much better to Bob than $60,000. They agreed to purchase the bus on credit, and by the time they were ready to pay for it and pick it up, enough money had come in to pay for the bus. But it was located on the West Coast, so there was the issue of getting it to New York, where the orphan choir would land.

Friends Gerald and Lureva Reynolds not only agreed to take the bus from California to meet the Romanian Orphan Choir in New York, but to stay with them as drivers across the country while they went from place to place.

When Bob first got the notion to tour the Romanian Orphan Choir, he was able to connect and schedule several choir appearances. Then he contacted longtime friend Connie Fortunato (now CEO of Music Camp International) to see if she could help. Connie had been doing special children's musical choirs as well as writing music curriculum, so Bob and Char felt she would be the perfect person to help set up the tour; she knew many people across the USA who might want to host this orphan choir. Connie, an exceptionally creative and organized person, agreed, and soon began setting up the tour which included singing on the steps of the Capitol building in Washington, DC.

It was a remarkable feat to put all of this together, with many moving parts. Not only did they do this the first time in 1995, but they have sponsored an orphan choir tour every year since then that raises sponsorships and funds to help support them!

Char said, "Some might think this is all a series of fortunate coincidences, but Bob and I know this is another one of those wonderful 'God things' we've seen happen over and over."

Consequently, for many years Assist International has been an integral part of the concept used for these orphan homes, a model that provides love and committed support that has helped orphaned children thrive. Seeing the success of this model encouraged Bob and Char to get involved to help establish orphan homes in other countries, as well.

The homes are not only in Oradea and other parts of Romania, but in various countries of Africa and as well as Thailand. The model consists of multi-bedroom neighboring homes, built in a large circle near each other that can house from eight to sixteen children with a couple trained as parents. Some of these parents also bring their biological children with them to live in these homes. Lars dedicated his life (alongside his previous wife Linda, who died of cancer several years ago) to help establish Caminul Felix. Lars's current wife Lisa has the same passion to see that abandoned children have loving homes; and together with Lars, their work is expanding to other countries.

Lars said, "Bob and Char Pagett have become people of incredible importance to those of us at Caminul Felix. Their love, compassion, and friendship have brought respect and awe, not only with our orphanage but with the government leaders here in Oradea. When we found land to build the second Caminul Felix Orphan Village, Bob became the chairman of the board and they stood by us the entire time, bringing the building teams and finances from the United States to build the new homes, ten homes in all. They also built the barn and found donors, including Foster Farms and dairy people from the East Coast to start the dairy farm, which now has four hundred milking cows that help feed our children in both orphanages and provide income by selling dairy products to the community. They are genuine people. Because of Bob and Char's love and ability to listen and treat us as friends, we have been able to accomplish much. They are people of the finest character we have ever met."

Assist International has made Caminul Felix Orphan Homes a high priority. There are now two separate campuses—one having six homes, the other having ten, for a total of sixteen homes. In addition, Assist International has helped build a teen house with apartments for young people who are transitioning into jobs or local colleges after turning eighteen. Assist International has built many of these homes plus several other buildings needed for schooling and training, in addition to a complete dairy farm that provides milk and cheese to both the orphan homes as well as sells milk and cheese to the community.

When Nancie and I were in Romania, we met many children and parents in the Caminul Felix homes who told us how their lives have been changed for the better. Seeing these homes and their parents reminded us of the power of seeing and helping the "one"—which multiplies into helping countless others.

It was a rare privilege to meet Marcel and Elli Filip, now directors of Caminul Felix Romania; and meet dedicated parents like Mihai and Nicoleta, Adrian and Angela, Mircea and Lidia, Emil and Simona, and dozens more who are giving their lives to love and parent these children. Bob and Char insist, "The house parents are the real heroes in this story."

As in any family, not all of it is easy, and there are deep wounds from abandonment as well as other issues. We asked Adrian and Angela what it takes for them to parent their nine children (two of them are their biological children).

"It takes patience," Angela said. "My goal is to teach them what a family is supposed to be and to lead them to have faith. I ask God every day, 'What can I do to help my children today?' Every day I pick it up and start over again. I emphasize respect, especially respect for oneself. I want them to know they have a right to an education and a responsibility to do something with their life. I pray every day, 'God, give us kids with good hearts.' If God did not help us, we could not do this."

While in Romania, we met an engaging young man named Razvan who drove us to various places. Razvan, a youth pastor, is married to Timea, who shared her story with us. Timea was five years old when her biological mother committed suicide. Her father, whom she did not know, was in jail. Her grandfather (whom she still visits) loved her but was ill and unable to care for her. Her grandfather heard about Caminul Felix and asked if they could take his granddaughter.

"At first, I did not like my new home. There were too many children," Timea said. "At that time, we had a full house of sixteen children, and I was afraid. But soon I started to enjoy my sisters and brothers. We took camping trips in the mountains and for the first time in my life, I had Christmas." She went on to tell us that she graduated from college with a degree in media and film, and that now she and Razvan have their first child. She said that every year, she and her orphan siblings (nine girls and fourteen boys) try to get together for a reunion. "We are truly brothers and sisters like any family, and we love to be together."

Arabela was five years old when she and her sister and brother were found eating out of garbage cans. She and her siblings were rescued and taken to a Caminul Felix Orphan home. Raised by loving parents in a home with sixteen children, she graduated from the University in Oradea with a degree in psychology. As is the character of Bob and Char, when Arabela invited them to her wedding they flew to Romania to attend. Arabela now has two children of her own. One by one, children in Romania were found, rescued, and given homes with loving and committed parents through Caminul Felix.

There are still thousands of orphans in Romania. We visited one state-run orphanage that had more than two hundred children, and we saw a marked difference in their behavior from the children at Caminul Felix. The children in the state-run orphanage clung to us, starved for personal touch. As we left, some followed us out to the entrance, clinging to us. One little boy, around nine years old, looked intensely at me. Without saying a word, his eyes begged me to take him home with me, which of course I could not do. We were heartbroken to leave these children, and I silently wept as we left. I could not help but think of my own grandchildren at home, so loved and wanted by their parents and all of us. We were told by one Romanian senator that there are still sixty thousand orphans in Romania. Some might argue that what Caminul Felix does for about two hundred kids is a drop in the bucket compared to the thousands of orphans. But if you visit with Cristiana, Arabela, Timea, or many others, you soon see that helping one life makes all the difference to that one.

The Immense Value in "One"

What is the dynamic power in seeing the one? It lies in seeing the immense value and potential of that one life. And this concept has rubbed off on the staff of Assist International.

Benjin Joshua, who is senior program manager of medical programs for Assist International, said, "One of our trainees was surprised with a birthday cake during a training session in Ethiopia. This was the first time this Ethiopian woman in her midthirties had been celebrated on her birthday. My team shared pictures of our trainee in tears and weeping as the class paused and our trainers sang for her. This seems like a small gesture. But I will forever cherish this memory of Assist International's 'focus on the one' value in action."

Ray Schmidt, former vice president of operations at Assist International, said, "I learned something from Char many years ago as I witnessed how she always focused on the 'one.' I would be wrapped up in getting a neonatal intensive care unit project completed and she was focused on the mothers with babies in the NICU, as one by one she gave them blankets and bottles for their newborns. She was motivated by the individual person, whereas I had been motivated by accomplishing the task. I learned that lesson early on and am grateful that this type of thinking has permeated Assist throughout the years. If we become centered on projects and programs, we risk losing focus on the 'one.' If the focus is on the individual, we sometimes will do things that may not make financial or even programmatic sense, but will end up positively impacting the orphan, the mother, or the patient."

When Bob and Char's granddaughter Sarah was born, she had serious complications and was placed in the intensive care nursery in Modesto, California. It just "so happened" that the nurse on duty was Betty Earle. She struck up a conversation with Bob and Char, who were there to see their baby granddaughter. Since Betty had worked in cardiac intensive care for many years, she was familiar with ICUs, monitors, and heart rhythms. Betty was fascinated to learn of Bob and Char's work with Assist International, and impulsively said, "I would love to go on one of your projects."

Now, twenty-one years later, Betty has completed more than twenty medical projects with Assist. Betty has caught the vision of seeing the "one"; and, through helping train people in other countries how to use the new medical equipment, she has seen lives saved. One life stands out.

It was a project in Zanzibar, at a hospital installing the island's first ICU which included a patient monitoring system, a telemetry monitoring system, and other related equipment and supplies. On the second day of the installation process, shortly after getting some of the monitors up and running, a crisis happened for a mother giving birth.

Char recalls having visited the maternity unit the night before when twins were born. But the next day Char noticed that the twins were listed as "orphaned," and she was told that the mother had died in the night. "The conditions were awful for the mothers," Char said. "They didn't even have sheets or enough beds. I watched two women laboring together on one mattress with no sheets, then after delivery sitting on the cement floor nursing their newborn babies. Then when they were dismissed from the hospital, they were wrapping their newborns in their skirts, as they had no blanket or anything for the new baby."

Ray Schmidt recalls that while they were continuing the installation, one of the hospital's nurses came running, grabbed him by the arm, and said he was needed immediately in the maternity ward because a mother who had just given birth was experiencing complications. "The nurse mistakenly thought I was a doctor, so I grabbed Betty Earle, our training nurse, and we rushed to the maternity unit," he said. Char quickly followed.

They found a woman on a bed, surrounded by eight or ten hospital staff, though no one was doing anything. The doctor who appeared to be in charge said the woman had experienced complications during the birth and that there was nothing that could be done. Everyone appeared hopeless as they stood around watching this woman die.

"Should I jump in and help?" Betty asked Ray.

"If you can, you should," he told her.

At that point, Betty Earle took over. "My first thought was that the mother was bleeding and I asked for a blood pressure," Betty said. "The nurses didn't have stethoscopes and weren't able to take a blood pressure. I checked her pulse, which was strong, but her color was very pale. There was no obvious bleeding. I started an intravenous line, as the nurses couldn't and the doctor who was there seemed unwilling.

"There was a problem with language and the doctor, who could speak some English, was interpreting for me as I spoke to the nurses. I asked for oxygen, and a large oxygen tank was brought in, but within five minutes the tank was empty."

The Assist International team had just completed the installation of some of the cardiac monitors in the labor and delivery unit the day before. Picture a large room with fifteen to twenty beds, with monitors installed at four of the beds. Betty instructed them to move the patient to one of the beds with a newly installed monitor.

"Now we could get oxygen saturation, blood pressure, and heart rhythm readings," Betty said. "What I found was the mother's blood pressure was extremely high, scary high. I turned to the doctor to ask what medications were available for hypertension, but the doctor now seemed to have trouble understanding me, and very reluctant to tell me what medications we could use."

"Since I wasn't about to let this woman stroke, I persisted," Betty said. "Finally, the doctor took me to her office and showed me a small package with six vials of atenolol, used to treat hypertension, a drug sent to them as a donation by another nonprofit group."

Ray added, "And then, after the drug was given, the anxious moments began to subside. The mother was stabilized. She was going to live. An audible cheer rose from the nurses. This was my first up-close experience with something like this, and tears flowed down my cheeks at this overwhelming experience where one life was saved."

Betty said, "The story had a happy ending as the last time I saw the patient she was stabilized and breast-feeding her baby."

Char often refers to her and Bob's passion of saving "one life"—that the much-needed medical equipment in developing and vulnerable countries can turn a "room of death" into a "room of life." One precious, valuable life saved.

What One Willing Person Can Do

If you can't feed a hundred people, then feed just one.

—**Mother Teresa**[37]

Making a difference begins with a first step. Whatever the first small step, it always starts where we are, with what we have and moves forward, including its ups and downs. And, when you step out to do something significant, it has influence on others to stretch their capabilities too.

Dana Hotton, who is now the director of finance at Assist International, had a dramatic experience in seeing how her life could make a difference. "When I first started working at Assist International, I helped with shipping. My supervisor left me an infant incubator needing to be shipped overseas, telling me it was crucial to get it out right away. I had never shipped anything international before, and at the time it was hard to get any help since most of the staff was traveling somewhere in the world. But I was determined and kept telling myself, 'How hard can this be?' As it turns out, it was a lot more complicated than I thought! It needed a commercial invoice, a packing slip, a letter of donation, including 'beneficiary information, a clearing agent, weights, dimensions,' etc.

"After a lot of effort, I ended up late on a Friday still not getting the incubator out. I finally pushed myself to call UPS and received permission to let me drive the incubator to them and bring my documents and get it shipped, even though it was after hours. A few weeks later, we received an email from the recipient doctor at the hospital where the incubator was sent. He said that the incubator saved a baby's life the very first day they received it! That's when it occurred to me that had I not pushed to get it out that late Friday and instead waited until the next week, at least one baby in this world would have died—and, for me, that was one too many. I had tears when I read his email and realized that even though I was not traveling as part of the boots on the ground, my small part of what was going on at Assist International helped save lives. At Assist, we have coined the term 'fingerprints' to describe this—our fingerprints are all over each project, each shipment, each program, each person."

How refreshing it is to realize that you are never too old to do things that you may have thought impossible! Sharon Fruh, professor and associate dean at the University of South Alabama College of Nursing, who is a member of the Assist International board of directors, tells this heartwarming story about her father:

"About ten years ago, the Caminul Felix Orphanage in Romania was doing a construction project. One of the teams that were supposed to take care of the cement work cancelled at the last minute. Bob called my husband and told him the predicament. My husband called my father to see if he and his team could help. My father quickly rallied his mission tradesmen who join my dad on all his concrete-work mission trips. They quickly raised money for the project and loaded up their tools and flew to Romania. The director of Caminul Felix who picked up my father and his skilled tradesmen from the airport was very worried when he saw the team and loaded them into the van. He called Bob and said, 'I think that Lars Svensson (my father) enlisted his workers from the rest home.' I must admit they were elderly, and my uncle Leif at that time used a cane. What the director did not realize was that these old crusty skilled Scandinavian craftsmen from Chicago were the best of the best in a lifetime of concrete work. The project was completed way ahead of schedule, and they even had time to put in sidewalks and extra projects for Caminul Felix. The director requested the team to return the following year. Never underestimate the power of senior citizens!"

Char said, "Good things can happen when we step out in faith and follow the passion and skill set that God has given us. And then, when willing to take the risks that are always inherent with faith, we can profoundly impact others. One of my favorite verses is, 'Trust in the Lord with all your heart, and lean not on your own understanding; in all your ways acknowledge Him, and God will direct your paths' (Prov. 3:5–6, NKJV)."

At a Caminul Felix board meeting in October 2019 at Oradea, Romania, Bob resigned as chairman of the board. Bob and Char knew it was time for new leadership for Caminul Felix to step in, but it was an emotional moment for them. They don't let go easily. All the memories flooded in of so many trips. . . of the dire circumstances they first had seen. . . of many children's lives changed for the better. Memories of hundreds of volunteers whose lives had also been changed by being involved, touching one life at a time.

Later that evening, there was a dinner for Bob and Char at the Noble House, a beautiful guest house that also functions as a gathering place. All the parents of the various orphan homes were at the special dinner, and it was a warm and inspirational time of honoring Bob and Char for their thirty years of leadership. Flowers were given to Char and a birthday cake to Bob, with much laughter and tears of joy and gratitude. Lars Hornberg addressed Bob and Char: "You have given such a big chunk of your lives to Caminul Felix. You caught the vision, and then shared the vision."

As I (Nancie) watched the moving series of meetings over the days in Romania of seeing Bob and Charlene in the setting where they had given so much, and received so much, I wondered, *How do they do this? How do they get so much done?* And Romania—although a powerful place that helped shape the mission of Assist International—is just part of the story of what is being accomplished. Other orphan homes in various countries of Africa, in Thailand. Desperately needed equipment in the neediest countries all over the world are provided. But it all started with seeing one person, one need.

Now, the work goes on. Michelle Sudfeld, Bob and Char's daughter and one of the directors of Assist International, also serves as chairman of the Caminul Felix board. She and her husband Ralph, who assumed the role of president of Assist International in 2015, have picked up the mantle of leadership.

I (Nancie) was moved to hear Michelle tell the story of Justin, a small boy of about six or seven (he does not know his age). His parents were killed in the civil war in Sudan, and he did not know what to do, so he just followed other refugees on foot across the border into Uganda. He found a safe shelter with Sister Rosemary and her team in Atiak (which we share more about in chapter 9). He was so happy to receive a pair of shoes. Michelle met him at the school commissioning in Atiak, where Assist International has built ten orphan homes, a school, and a nearly completed medical clinic. They are also in the process of constructing a dining common. When Michelle showed me the pictures of Justin, my heart melted, too—a little boy small for his age but so happy to have found a place of belonging, wearing his new red and blue school uniform—and of course, his new shoes. Michelle said, "I will never forget him, watching him sing of the love of the Lord, and quoting Scripture."

While you and I may not be called to go to other countries, there is something we can do, each one of us. We can give much-needed financial support. We can also open our eyes to needs right where we are.

Here in the United States, we have thousands of homeless children, some sleeping on the streets or in cars, and thousands more being passed from foster home to foster home. We have single parents trying to survive. No matter where we live, there are people right now who need to be seen, who need help. And in doing so, we can change one life.

Mahatma Gandhi once said, "In a gentle way, you can shake the world." Those who find meaning in loving others, even in difficult and vulnerable places, are the happiest and most fulfilled people on earth. David Brooks quotes Anne Colby and William Damon of Stanford University, who studied people who have found meaning: "There's not a lot of moral reflection that goes into the choice to give yourself away. . . . There are not a lot of internal battles or adding up the costs and benefits. Instead, we saw an unhesitating will to act, a disavowal of fear and doubt, and a simplicity of moral response. The risks were ignored, and consequences were un-weighed."[38]

Char said, "I came to realize that it's the one person you're with at the moment that's important. When you personally interact with individuals, one by one you see them, love them, and touch them. It is very gratifying for me to approach humanitarian work this way. Maybe those reading this book cannot go overseas and do what we do. But if you can reach a neighbor with love by providing them with a warm meal when they are sick, or sitting with a mother who is grieving over the death in their family, or because they're going through a divorce and you can be there for them, that one person is valuable to God and even what little you may feel you have to share with them can make all the difference."

We all want to succeed but we tend to quantify it: What is our annual budget? How many sales did we make? How many books have we sold? How many projects have we completed? How many members do we have? How much money did we make?

Many people today feel powerless, but they do not realize the power they have as one person. You may ask: Is it possible for one life, one person, to do extraordinary things? The answer is an emphatic YES. Bob and Char Pagett have lived that principle, and the results are bearing fruit.

The life of faith has a different economy: Is the life of one person changed for the better because of my influence?

The "magic" of Bob and Char's lives is that they have focused on the one person, the one task placed in front of them. Oswald Chambers said, "The people who influence us most are not those who buttonhole us and talk to us, but those who live their lives like the stars in heaven and the lilies in the field, perfectly simply and unaffectedly. Those are the lives that mold us."[39]

CHAPTER EIGHT

THE POWER OF NETWORKING

You can make more friends in two months by becoming interested in other people than you can in two years by trying to get other people interested in you.

—Dale Carnegie[40]

Bob Pagett has an uncanny ability to network. It helps that he and Char are faithful and loyal "joiners." They show up for their people—whether it's a class reunion, their ministerial association, through social events with friends and extended family. Maybe it's even through connecting with someone at a memorial service, a wedding, a graduation. Not one connection is wasted, because the force of love is behind their connections. We have seen it happen. After a wedding reception of one of our own children, Bob somehow connected with one of our nephews, who ended up going on an international trip with him. But this happens all the time. It's their modus operandi.

They are passionate about loving God and loving people. And underlying it all is their vision to meet the needs of the most vulnerable of the world.

In many of the projects Bob and Char have done, it was through connections in their network—their churches, friends, colleagues, Rotary friends, friends of friends—people they met "along the way." And somehow, they end up connecting with donors, supporters, and missionaries in obscure parts of the world, networking needs with resources.

Effective networking is fueled by how we see people. Do we see a person as an object (a means to our end), or as someone uniquely and wonderfully made, with God-given potential and talents? Effective, lasting networking lies in how we see people.

Bob Goff said, "Loving people isn't a strategy; when it has an agenda, it isn't love anymore."[41] The German theologian Martin Buber expanded on this principle in his classic book *I and Thou*.[42] How essential it is to see the "thou," the sacred spark of the Creator, in others. How essential it is to see a person as someone of worth instead of someone to use.

The power of networking expands when we connect with others who also want to make a difference. It is said, "to whom much is given, much shall be required." When we realize how much we have compared to others who are in need simply because of their circumstances, a sense of justice and a calling to make a difference compels us to act.

We can learn a lot from other people. We see mistakes we can correct. We see ways to get better, more effective, especially when we don't care who gets the credit. Networking is an immensely empowering principle that takes place in many ways; at times unconsciously, and is a byproduct of all the other associations of whatever field of interest we are involved in.

But networking starts with a basic principle: reaching out in friendship. An old proverb says, "If a man would have friends, he must show himself friendly." Networking can be as basic and simple as greeting someone you do not know, reaching out to introduce yourself. Listening to her. Listening to his story-within-a-story. Finding the common interest, and seeing others as an ally, not a competitor.

While Char is the most gracious and hospitable person you could imagine, Bob is the chief networker. In observing for many years how Bob has done this, I (Bill) came to realize that the key for Bob was not trying to get people interested in what he wanted to accomplish, but discovering what others wanted to accomplish. And when he found someone who wanted to accomplish something for some of the world's most vulnerable people, he found in them a likeness of purpose.

When you couple this quality with Bob's willingness to say yes to almost anything that will meet his goal of helping the world's most vulnerable, and Char's gift of attention to detail, it's understandable how he and Char have been able to accomplish so much.

An example of this is from a previously referenced story about Dr. Ion Patrascu, whom Bob helped come to America to tell his story to raise awareness and funds to help orphans in Romania suffering from AIDS. The people in the United States who heard Dr. Patrascu give his presentation contacted Assist International; The result of connections through networking is that the University of Cluj Medical Center in Romania not only got cardiac care monitors, but they also got biomed engineers to set them up and to train local biomed engineers to run them.

Bob said, "It's just a God thing how these things come together to help the world's most vulnerable." This is no doubt true, but it is also Bob's talent of persistently telling the story until the story clicks with the right people, who bring the right pieces to the puzzle to get the project done. And once Bob says yes, Char—usually behind the scenes in the early years, was the logistics person who organized the shipping until Ray Schmidt, who was an answer to prayer for Char!—was on board.! In the early days Charlene booked the flights and accommodations, distributed finances, and handled all the other details needed, including packing Bob's suitcase, to get the project from point A to point B. Those of us who know Bob just smile and say, "You can't make this up!" But it worked for him and Char, even when they had a small staff—or no staff at all. Now that the younger staff has taken over, the principle of networking continues even more.

Over the years, Assist International has become more stream-lined, setting criteria more in tune with professionals they work with, and have developed criteria to carefully research projects before they begin. But the basic principle of networking with oth-ers and finding out what their goals are, and then fitting what Assist International does to those goals (if it meets Assist Interna-tional's overall objective of helping the world's most vulnerable), still holds true.

How to Effectively Network

Here are some principles we have observed on how Bob and Char build relationships with others. These are simple yet profound principles that bear fruit.

Genuinely Love People

> *If we have no peace, it is because we have forgotten*
> *that we belong to each other.*

> **—Mother Teresa**[43]

When you love someone, you show interest in what they do and what they need. Char's youngest brother Jim, when asked what is most memorable about them, said, "I have always looked up to them as leaders and mentors. They have been the highest examples of love, kindness, generosity, and friendship. They simply care about people and will always go the second mile to be a part of your life. They are driven to touch people's lives with love and friendship."

Jim went on to say, "In addition to flying all over the world meeting the needs of the poor, they are the aunt and uncle at every family wedding, graduation, and as many birthdays as they can possibly get to. They drove almost six hundred miles (one way) to surprise me on my fortieth birthday. They came to all my kids' graduations and weddings, but it's not just my kids, it's all the cousins too and we are a big family. They are amazing!"

Love means focused attention—noticing people and listening to what's going on in their lives. We all know people who are more interested in themselves than in anyone else. Someone I used to see occasionally at a book convention I attended would come up to me and say, "Hi Bill, how are you?" As I said hello and began to speak, rather than looking at me and showing interest in what I was saying, I would watch his eyes wander out in the crowd of people, seeing if there was someone else he would rather be talking to. It gave me the sense that he did not care about me or anything I might say. But I confess I have probably done the same at times, being distracted by checking messages on my phone instead of noticing the person right in front of me. For all of us, having actual face-to-face conversations with others—with sustained attention—takes continual intention these days.

Benjin Joshua tells his personal story, showing that loving others is not just a policy with Assist International in terms of their outreach but exists in real time with the staff:

"We get so focused on the people we are helping externally. I forgot how well we love each other internally at Assist International until I went through a divorce in 2017. I found myself in a very dark season of my life. I lost twenty-five pounds in six weeks, going 24-to-36–hour periods without sleep or food.

"It was during this season I saw a side of Assist International staff and leadership that I found hard to accept. People loved me unconditionally, created space for me to heal, and journeyed alongside me as best as they could while rolling out programs all over the world. People don't see this often, but we love each other at Assist International just as passionately and intentionally as the people we serve externally."

Phil Callaway wrote, "There is no better friendship booster than the ability to listen. The ability to show genuine interest in others is an admirable quality of a true friend."[44]

To be honest, listening to others is not always easy. Sometimes we would rather be with more exciting people, or with others who could enhance us. There is nothing magical in learning to listen, but it is a discipline we all can grow in. David Augsburger wrote, "Being heard is so close to being loved that for the average person, they are almost indistinguishable."[45] People know if you care about them, and listening is a profound way to express it. Bob Goff says, "Most people need love and acceptance a lot more than they need advice."[46]

Go the Second Mile

You go the first mile; you discharge a duty; you go the second mile, and you make a friend. The great men and women in history have been those willing to go the second mile.

—Dr. Beverly Chiodo[47]

Ligia Dugulescu, Peter's Dugulescu's daughter, was eighteen at the time of the Romanian revolution. We told the story of how she was in Timisoara Square as she watched her father go up to the stage to speak. Tears ran down her face as she was terrified, wondering if she were watching her father for the last time, fearing he would be executed by the communistic regime of Romania. Thank God he was not and went on to help rebuild his country.

For seven years, Ligia worked with her father. By then, Bob and Char had made multiple trips to Romania and had become not just a major factor in helping JHOR Orphanage program, but had become close friends of the Dugulescu family, as well as the people at Caminul Felix Orphan compounds.

Then suddenly in 2008, as Peter was driving to an appointment, he felt pains in his chest and pulled his car to the side of the road. He was alone and having a heart attack. Someone called for help, but by the time the ambulance arrived, Peter had passed away.

Peter's sudden death was a shock to Ligia and her family. Once again, she was panicked, wondering what would happen to their organization now that her father was gone. She was concerned that no one else could provide the leadership or fund-raising that Peter was so capable of doing. She felt that while the responsibility fell to her, she was not capable of continuing without her father.

Ligia did not understand why God would take her father. Her mother encouraged her to hold steady. "Ligia, people come and go, but God stays," her mother said. They prayed for wisdom and for their team. The orphan children prayed too, for fear of going back on the streets.

"Bob Pagett was the first person I called," Ligia said. "Immediately, Bob wired us $20,000 and booked a flight for both he and Char to get to Romania as fast as they could." Thousands mourned Peter's death. He was buried in the Cemetery of Revolutionary Heroes in Timisoara. And Bob and Char were right there with Ligia, her mother, and her younger sister through it all.

"While my mother told me 'People come and go,' that is not true about Bob and Char. In a sense, Bob has replaced my dad to me. Bob and Char were there for us and continue to this day to be there for us," Ligia said.

After the burial, Eunice, the younger sister of Ligia, asked Bob and Char, "Will you be my godparents?" They said yes, not really knowing what was required of them. But they kept in close touch with her, expressing their love and support.

When Eunice became engaged to a young man going to medical school, she called Bob. "Since you lost a daughter and I lost my dad, will you walk me down the aisle at my wedding?"

So it was that in the summer of 2009, Bob and Char flew to Romania, taking their twelve-year-old granddaughter Juliana with them for Eunice's wedding. "There were tears of both joy and sadness," Char explained, "tears of joy for Eunice, tears of sadness that her father, Peter, was not there to give her away." Bob was able to give Eunice's hand in marriage to her husband Christian at their beautiful wedding. Christian completed his internship and now works as a medical doctor in Baden-Baden, Germany.

Bob and Char live the principle that a valuable part of networking goes far beyond the people you connect with on websites like LinkedIn or Facebook. True networking carries with it a sense of empathy, connection, and commitment.

Daniel H. Pink wrote, "Empathy is about standing in someone else's shoes, feeling with his or her heart, seeing with his or her eyes. Not only is empathy hard to outsource and automate, but it makes the world a better place."[48] Empathy is a hallmark of how Bob and Char network with others, whether it is the people who go with them to projects or the recipients like Ligia and Eunice who feel cared for and loved. Bob and Char genuinely want to share life with the people they pull into their circle. You are not just a resource to them; you are a friend and brother or sister. Loving others—really loving—means getting involved with them.

Best-selling author Dr. Bernie Siegel said, "Studies of volunteers have shown there is a benefit to performing acts of love for other people. The irony is that it is in your best interest to be selfless. The things you do for the benefit of others not only make you feel fulfilled, but they also increase your chances of living a long and happy life. Remember that an act of love always benefits at least two people."[49]

Take Action

> **The worst sin toward our fellow creatures is not to hate them, but to be indifferent to them: that's the essence of inhumanity.**
>
> **—George Bernard Shaw**[50]

It's not just loving people—Bob and Char are notorious for providing actual concrete help to others. If they can't help you, they will try to find someone else who can. Someone once told me that Bob is "like a pit bull. Once he says yes to help, he does not let go until he finds a way to get it done." Bob and Charlene's daughter Michelle adds that Bob has been often teased that "Assist International" can at times become "*In*sist International" because of his perseverance to help those in need.

I (Bill) recall a phone conversation with Dr. Bert Parks, one of the authors we have published through Deep River Books. Dr.

Parks is a renowned neurosurgeon in the States and has written a book about his volunteer work in Kenya, Africa, trying to help train doctors at the local hospital. He told me about his frustration in trying to find a CT scanner, which was crucial not only to the training he was doing, but crucial for the patients in Kenya and the surrounding African countries that had none.

"I've tried every source I know for the past several years. There just seems to be zero interest in the medical world in helping us get this equipment, probably because CT scanners cost so much," he'd said. "We don't have the funds to buy one and I've pretty much given up."

I told him I knew someone who might be able to help. He laughed and said, "Trust me, it is pretty much impossible, and I'd hate for you to waste your time." When I hung up the phone, I called Bob Pagett.

After telling Dr. Parks' story to Bob, he replied, "Wow, Bill, this could be the mother of all projects! Do you know how much they cost?" I had no idea how much a CT scanner cost, being a medical novice. (I later found out that a new high-end scanner is in the high six- to seven-figure range.)

"Well, I know they aren't cheap," I said, "but Dr. Parks tells me this would make Tenwick Hospital in Kenya a neurological center for about seven countries in Africa. Right now, they have none."

I think that was all it took. After a short pause, Bob said, "Well, I'll see what I can find out, but there is no guarantee." I hung up the phone, knowing that Bob would go to work to try to find one, thinking that if anyone on the planet could find a donated CT scanner, it would be "Yes-Bob, the pit bull."

Later, I asked Bob to tell me how he went about trying to find a CT scanner. "First of all, I called Dr. Parks, introduced myself, and asked him more about his work in Kenya. I also needed more information about the hospital, and a list of doctors who were on the staff," he said. "I also had to prepare a report as to why this project was important, taking a cue from Dr. Bert Parks as to why the CT scanner was needed. Once I had that information, I started knocking on doors. It was a process to find a donor that would agree to donate such a large piece of equipment.

"In this process, I discovered that even if I found one, Assist International would need to take ownership of it. Assist International would have to not only assume legal liability but cost for installation and the build out of a new section of the hospital for the equipment. Also, someone would have to provide the ongoing maintenance costs which are quite extensive."

Bob left no stone unturned to find a CT scanner that would be available as a donation. It turned out to be quite a challenge. Most people would give up at this point. But not "Yes-Bob, the pit bull!"

One hospital in Northern California had partnered with Assist International on more than fifteen international projects. Bob decided to inquire about any contacts that the hospital had with some of their major medical equipment providers. It was through this network of relationships that Bob was put in contact with a company that had a CT scanner that they were willing to make available for this project in Kenya.

The hospital CEO joined with Bob in the effort, and Bob did a powerful job communicating the great need in Kenya and the story of the Tenwek Hospital. And together, they secured the donation of a CT scanner to the Tenwek Hospital in Bomet, Kenya.

A miracle was happening. When we called Dr. Parks, he was stunned. He could *not* believe Bob had accomplished this in a few weeks, when he had been trying and praying for this for years.

After telling the story many times, Bob succeeded in raising additional funds, while Dr. Parks and other doctors agreed to raise finances needed for the service agreement with local Kenyan service technicians and the cost of consumables. In addition, the Tenwek Hospital raised additional funding for a newly engineered building to house the CT scanner. An illustration of networking at its finest.

The project has been a resounding success. Bob said, "Tenwek Hospital is a hospital that is made of core doctors from some of the top medical schools in the USA working alongside some of the finest 'in-country' physicians. No one goes under the knife without prayer before surgery."

Today, Tenwek Hospital is a 361-bed hospital that serves about 600,000 people within a thirty-two-kilometer radius. It is now a surgery referral center for the entire region of more than 8.5 million people. More than five thousand operations are performed annually. Out in front of the hospital, on the major highway leading to the hospital, is a sign that says, "WE TREAT, JESUS HEALS."

Bob "the networker" did it again, even though he and Assist International took no credit. At the commissioning Bob let everyone know that the heroes were Dr. Parks, the corporation that donated the CT scanner, and all the others who contributed to the success of this project.

Tell the Story

> *Just as despair can come to one only from other human beings, hope too, can be given to one only by other human beings.*

> **—Elie Wiesel**[51]

When I asked Bob how he asks for support for these projects, he said, "Usually I just tell stories about what is happening and what the needs are. Then I invite key people to come with me to a specific place where the need is. I've taken pastors, Rotarians, doctors, donors, and many others on trips to parts of the world they had never experienced before. Some catch the vision and get involved."

When we were doing research for this book, one Assist International volunteer said, "Bob was in my city and invited me to have coffee with him. He told me a story that genuinely moved me, then invited me to go with him to the Romanian Orphan project he had described." The volunteer smiled and said, "That turned out to be the most expensive cup of coffee I ever had."

This goes back to the concept of empathy. When you hear a story, as Bob so often tells of a need someplace in the world, it can move some people enough to give a donation or pray for the people needing help. But when that person goes with Bob and Char, sees the people, and experiences their lives, it can make a life-changing difference.

Betty Earle, the nurse from Modesto, California who has been on many medical projects with Assist International, says, "Bob and Char have greatly inspired me and changed the way I view the world. For one thing, I am incredibly grateful for the life I have lived. When I was growing up, I always thought we were poor. Turns out I didn't know what poverty was. You can't travel to these poorer countries and not have it make you more grateful. I am proud to be a small part of this amazing organization run by people who care."

Many of the volunteers who have been on multiple trips to do a project with Assist International say that their first experience hooked them. Their lives and empathy for others was forever changed.

Give Credit to Your Partners

*It is amazing what you can accomplish if you do not
care who gets the credit.*

—Harry S. Truman[52]

In Africa there is a concept known as *ubuntu*—the profound sense
that we are human only through the humanity of others; that if
we are to accomplish anything in this world it will in equal measure be due to the work and achievement of others. *Ubuntu* is a
basic principle of Assist International. After every project there is
a dedication ceremony and Bob and Char are almost always there
at the ceremony, giving credit to the organizations and people
who have made the project possible. Bob loves plaques and has
been famous for giving plaques since he was a youth director in
Oregon. Only God knows how many plaques Bob has given to
credit those who have helped achieve success in various projects.

Anyone who has ever listened to Bob tell a story of a finished
project will never hear him say "I did this"; instead, you will hear
him talk about the "outstanding" or "dynamic" other people
who have worked with him to accomplish it. He and Char have
a unique way of making everyone around them feel special,
appreciated, and affirmed. And it's genuine. They really feel that
the people God brings into their lives are gifts from God.

The Power of Affirmation

*There is a grace of kind listening, as well as a grace
of kind speaking. . . . Kind words are the music
of the world.*

—Frederick Wm. Faber[53]

The word "affirm" means to validate and to state positively. Practically, this defines a nurturing communications style, one in which you talk to yourself and to others in a positive manner. This is a natural part of how Bob and Char communicate, and most everyone who you talk to will say that being with them makes them feel heard and affirmed. They come away from being with Bob and Char feeling "special."

Bob and Char do this by implementing spontaneous praise. It is not flattery (which is hollow praise to manipulate), but a genuine affirmation of a person. Every so often, and out of the blue, I will get a text or email from Bob in which he says, "Bill, I love you like my own brother. You are one of the most gifted people I know, and I am so grateful for you." I usually feel a bit embarrassed when I read that or hear him say it in person, especially since I recall the moments of grief I gave him as a twelve-year-old kid while he was courting my sister. But coming from Bob, and even though I personally doubt that I am one of the "most gifted people he knows" given the amazing people he knows, I recognize that his words are genuine and come from his heart, and I feel affirmed regarding what skills I do have.

Bob and Char would be the first to agree that they are not perfect. They are just as human as all of us, and everyone has times of anger and frustrations, and they are no exception. But what a great skill it is to cultivate the art of listening to others and affirming another person.

The Immense Value of Relationships

If you want to go fast, go alone. If you want to go far, go together.

—African Proverb

Understanding the importance of good relationships is the most powerful asset an individual or an organization can have. Relationships affect everything—from the White House to the United Nations; to universities and company board rooms; to churches and small businesses; and especially within communities, neighborhoods, and families. If we value and cultivate good relationships (which really is networking at its finest), we have a tremendous asset. Bob and Char have prioritized relationships all their lives, and consequently have a powerful network.

Relationships need cultivating, and everyone needs a bit of affirmation or encouragement from time to time. Giving affirmation is a skill that you can learn. A couple of years ago my New Year's resolution was to try to say words of affirmation to someone every day. It has proven to give me a personal sense of gratification.

When I (Nancie) was doing research for a book, I surveyed more than two hundred people and asked them, "Who made a difference in your life?" I was expecting to hear famous, notable people mentioned. Instead, the response was: mothers, fathers, aunts, teachers. Mentors. In other words, key people in their lives. Each one of us is a "key" person to someone. What a powerful gift we can give to show love and kindness to those in our lives.

Each of us have a network of people, and each of us can offer love, affirmation, and encouragement to those within our network. When we notice the good work and actions of others, no matter how small, it can make an enormous difference. The Greek meaning for "encouragement" means "to urge forward." It doesn't take much—just awareness as we open our eyes to see the possibilities of amazing things happen as we widen the circle. We can do so much more together than on our own.

Bob and Char have practiced the powerful concepts of networking to reach out to the world's most vulnerable. And through strength of relationships, care enough about people to offer a cup of cold water in Jesus's name. It also means generously sharing the vision with others, and in doing so, see amazingly beautiful things happen.

Life is short, and we have never too much time
for gladdening the hearts of those who are traveling
the dark journey with us. Oh, be swift to love,
make haste to be kind!

—Henri F. Amiel[54]

CHAPTER NINE

EMPOWERING ANOTHER'S DREAM

*Give me a lever long enough and a fulcrum on which
to place it, and I shall move the world.*

—Archimedes

Empowering another's dream allows you to achieve more by working with others. Lars Hornberg, founder of the Caminul Felix Orphanages in Oradea, Romania, said of Bob and Char, "There is no competitiveness with them, no competition regarding who the work derives from. They are like old friends who provide not only resources, but their love and friendship. They came into our lives when we were alone in this, and they believed in us."

Empowering or leveraging another's dream is a powerful concept that is familiar to all of us. Parents and grandparents spend big chunks of their lives trying to help their children and grandchildren see their dreams realized. What do any of us have that we have not been given? Really, nothing—and when we can pay it forward, what we give grows exponentially. Beyond our dreams, even.

Martin Luther King had a dream to see racial justice in our time. Although his life came to a tragic early end, his dream of bringing justice to oppressed people lives on and his dream continues to empower many others' dreams.

In the case of Bob and Char Pagett, it means coming alongside someone already doing something innovative and helpful, and helping them to be even more effective. It is servant leadership at its finest. A key ingredient in much of the work that Assist International has done has been the ability to find others who are doing something significant, and then come alongside them to help make the dream a reality. Many humanitarian organizations tend to want to control the projects they fund, as well as get the credit. But Bob and Char have found their success in seeing others succeed.

As a wise man said, "One standing alone can be attacked and defeated, but two can stand back-to-back and conquer; three is even better, for a triple-braided cord is not easily broken" (Eccl. 4:12, TLB).

Empowering another's dream or project helps build something lasting. Not only does it not "reinvent the wheel," it also provides on-the-ground stability to the mission. But true empowerment is done in a way that, while influencing some direction and resources, does not try to control or "own" their dream.

The Key to Empowering Someone Else

At the end of the day, it's not about what you have
or even what you've accomplished. . . it's about who
you've lifted up, who you've made better.

—Denzel Washington[55]

Empowering another involves these qualities:

- *Discernment.* Recognizing another's talent and effectiveness and see how you can help. Some projects may fit your own mission statement, and some may not. It's important to discern which ones do.

- *Maturity.* Big ideas require "big people" in order to address big dreams. Effective leveraging requires being secure enough in yourself that you are willing to invest in another's dream because you see that it has value, and you realize that together, you can get more done.

- *Willingness to risk.* You may not be entirely sure how it will work out, but you are willing to try. Is there a chance you will get burned? Yes—but it's worth the risk. After all, someone took a chance on us one time.

- *Generosity.* Above all, empowering another takes generosity—not only generosity with money and donors, but simply generosity of spirit—wanting to see another dream succeed, for the sake of Christ's calling of love for all.

Relationships are crucial to effectively leveraging another's dream. It must be a win-win. Helping other people's work means helping them succeed, which is also compatible with your own goals.

Senator Mitt Romney said, "For American foreign aid to become more effective, it must embrace the power of partnerships and the transformative nature of free enterprise and leverage the abundant resources that can come from the private sector."[56] Bob and Char have made the concept of empowering others a prominent feature of their work. If there is a secret to their success, this is it: empowering another's dreams, especially when they are doing God's work of helping the poor and needy of the world.

The partnerships they have developed, both with resources here in the United States as well as in various countries of the world, have not only been a more efficient way to accomplish their goals but have provided the way for others to also fulfill their calling. *It is astounding to consider that the nonprofit Bob and Char started has completed more than six hundred projects in sixty-five countries.* But it began with one project, one person at a time—and it continues with one at a time. The amazing thing is that one project tends to create an effective "network" dynamic that brings other projects to Assist International. Leveraging another's dreams also leverages your own. When you give, you receive.

The following stories of these three humanitarian leaders in Uganda illustrate the power of leveraging another's dream: Sam Tushabe, Bob and Carol Higgins, and Sister Rosemary.

Sam Tushabe's Story

If you want to go somewhere, it is best to find someone who has already been there.

—Robert Kiyosaki[57]

Cheri and Tim Reynolds were attending a church that hosted a young man named Sam Tushabe, who had committed his life to helping orphaned and vulnerable children in his homeland of Uganda. The meeting was God-ordained, because Assist International was at a point where it was ready to expand its involvement with organizations in Africa that were caring for orphaned and vulnerable children in need. Through this connection, Sam was introduced to Bob and Char, who shared a similar vision to help children in Uganda and a great partnership was formed.

Sam's concept was a dream to build a model orphanage similar to Caminul Felix, but he wanted to take it a step further to provide intensive training to both the orphans and potential new parents so they could someday be self-sufficient. His philosophy was to "give a hand up, not a handout." But his dream was in obvious need of a partner.

Sam told Bob and Char his story. As a young child, Sam's father abandoned the family, and to keep herself and the family alive, his mother would go into the forest and collect wood to sell. Sadly, Sam's father had given Sam's mother the HIV virus and she became deathly ill. Sam tried his best to take care of her and his sister. As she was nearing death she told Sam, who was by now about twelve years old, that he must get an education.

At the time, it seemed impossible to Sam. After she died, he survived by gathering wood just as his mother had done, to help him and his sister get food. But he was determined to fulfill his mother's wish and go to school. He not only continued to gather wood, but he cleaned the local school, sleeping on the porch of the school at times, and doing any job he could find.

Amazingly, he did this through high school. After completing his basic education, he was introduced to a group called Youth with a Mission (YWAM). He joined the group for training and was sent to Kenya, Africa for further studies. While in Kenya, he noticed children trying to survive by gathering food and other things from a local garbage dump. Being an orphan himself, it triggered something inside of him, and helping orphaned children became his passion.

He returned to Uganda to see what he could do. One day Sam was standing in line to purchase groceries and overheard a woman crying to her friend that she had adopted so many family members and that another relative had just passed away, but she did not have the money to take in another child. Sam, an orphan himself, felt burdened for this child. He spoke up and told the woman in front of him, "If you raise the child, I will find the money to support the child."

All around him were families who were leaving orphan children behind due to the AIDS epidemic. Sam began by supporting one orphan. He did this by creating greeting cards he would sell and doing other odd jobs, eventually supporting as many orphans as he could, always making sure they got to school. Sam, as it turns out, was a true entrepreneur, and his ideas and businesses grew.

He married Nancy, a nurse he had met during his YWAM days, and by the time he met Bob and Char, Sam was supporting more than two hundred orphan children by finding foster homes and sending these kids to school. He was also teaching women to sew to be able to support themselves.

In the meantime, a businesswoman who had gone to Romania with A.I. and helped build one of the orphan homes at Caminul Felix expressed a desire to help other orphan children and ended up donating some stock from the company she worked for to A.I. for this purpose.

By now, Sam Tushabe had founded an organization called AIDS Orphan Education Trust (AOET). He had already established an elementary school, a medical clinic, and a primitive space under a thatched roof where kindergarten was being held. Sam had purchased ten acres of land, although that land was landlocked.

Bob Pagett, Tim Reynolds, and Chris Carmichael went out to Uganda to visit Sam Tushabe and the work he had already established. Assist International saw the potential in Sam Tushabe and his AOET dream, and the effective leadership that Sam and his wife Nancy provided. They decided to help AOET by purchasing an additional ten acres, which gave AOET access to the main road in Jinja, Uganda, where Sam dreamed of having family homes and a high school.

As of this writing, through the substantial donations of caring people, churches and other organizations, several houses have been built, as well as a dormitory, fruit farm, high school, and fresh-water wells. The work at AOET has now grown to twenty-three family homes where several orphans are cared for by foster parents in each home. There is a new high school, three dormitories for students who attend the school, a purified water system, and more campuses.

AOET now reaches more than four thousand children. The concept of "a hand up, not a handout" is explained this way: any couple who wants to become parents in one of the orphan homes will be able to live in the home with their biological family for up to five years, supported fully by AOET. It will include educational and vocational training for the parents as well as the children. But they also must be willing to accept, love, and parent the orphan children being placed in the home. The father in the home needs to have a full-time job, with the money earned being dedicated to savings, to earn enough to purchase their own home within five years, and then moving with both their biological and orphan children into their own home. Eventually, the AOET home will then repeat the process with new parents and new orphans.

By leveraging Sam's dream, the work of AOET has expanded not only in Uganda but also in Kenya, Zambia, Botswana, and Rwanda, helping thousands of African orphaned children have a new lease on life and helping hundreds of parents of these homes get new vocational training so they can find better jobs to support their families.

Many women in Africa are not educated or trained, and if their husband dies or leaves them, by custom, the husband's side of the family can come and take everything, leaving the widows destitute, without means to feed and clothe her children. It sounds unfair and archaic, which it is, but cultural habits and traditions are hard to change. Many of these women are also responsible for their own parents. Without vocational training or jobs, their situations can be desperate, and they and their children can suffer unimaginably. Cheri Reynolds, daughter of Bob and Char, saw this problem and decided to help by establishing small cottage-type industries for them. Now, these women are creating beautiful jewelry that is sold in the United States to provide sustenance for them and their families and giving them some sense of empowerment.

Another example of African women's empowerment through Assist International would be the ovens that were purchased and sit at the edge of the village; women can sign up to use one of them for two hours each day. They can bake Queen Cakes, bread, and other goods, and sell them in the marketplace. Sewing machines are also provided for women to make and sell clothing and school uniforms. These wonderful projects help these women's children go to school and not be hungry when going to bed.

Bob and Carol Higgins' Story

In the summer of 2007 Assist International became aware of Bob and Carol Higgins working in Lira, in northern Uganda. Bob and Carol were retired schoolteachers from Bend, Oregon. Carol had been a home economics teacher; Bob was in wood-shop vocational training. Following their teaching careers, they became pastors in

Alfalfa, Oregon. In some ways, they were like Bob and Charlene, having felt led by God to reach out to the most vulnerable in poorer parts of the world and take their skills to help.

Their work in Uganda began as a ministry for training pastors and leaders. They had not come to Uganda to help with orphans. In fact, Bob Higgins once famously said, "We don't do orphans." But God sometimes has other plans, and what may appear to us as a distraction can be the main agenda.

A couple of the Ugandan pastors Bob and Carol Higgins were working with said, "We have a group of orphans that we'd like you to meet. So, we agreed to visit them," Carol said. "We met this ragtag bunch of over fifty children, crammed together in a small house. Up to six children were having to share one plate of food, maybe every third day, and were forced to share small mats, one blanket for six kids for sleeping. They were barely surviving."

Some of the children had witnessed the Lord's Resistance Army[58] killing their parents in raids, and some of their parents had died of AIDS. Like many children in war-torn areas, these vulnerable children had no place to go for help.

Carol told us, "At that meeting, in addition to the children, some regional commissioners were there as well. The kids had prepared a program for us with singing. I thought, 'What's this?' It became obvious that this was a presentation in hopes that we would get involved to help." Bob continued telling the story: "It was a big deal. And we kind of had our heads in the sand and didn't really understand what was going on. So we left some money for them to buy a bag of beans."

Every week, there was a little bit of contact over the next several months, and Bob and Carol would send them a little bit of money for some food. "Really, we had almost no contact or interaction," Carol said. "And then we were having a board meeting with our leaders and one of them said, 'You know, those kids consider you to be their sponsor.'

"We didn't have any experience, we didn't have any budget, we didn't have a major church behind us, we didn't have a foundation, we didn't have a trust. We thought, if we make this commitment and if the money doesn't come in, we've still got orphans to feed," Carol said. "So, I was very reluctant to make a commitment to say yes, we'll take this on."

But it was even harder for Bob and Carol to ignore the precious children. Eventually they realized that God wanted them to try to do something. Sometimes it can be agonizing to say yes to what God is asking of us. We tend to see the overwhelming problem rather than focusing on God's provision. The walk of faith is always a challenging one, but it was a faith opportunity for Bob and Carol Higgins, who saw the challenge before them and knew they would need to rely on God's provision.

They began to look for some property where they might build an orphanage to house these kids. They came back to the States to try to raise some money, and eventually they were able to buy a twelve-acre piece of land. The plan then was to clear the land and raise some additional money to build some orphan homes. But things became urgent before they had been able to construct anything.

The terrible Lord's Resistance Army had invaded a refugee camp nearby, leaving hundreds of orphans. The word got back to Bob and Carol that the LRA was planning to come back and capture the children as "trainees" for the LRA. But the Higginses managed to find a large dump truck and sent some of those working with them to bring about eighty of the children to Lira.

They had no facilities yet, so they went to the local grade school in Lira. The school agreed to accommodate the children for three months, reserving two large rooms for them to sleep, and would feed them and enroll them in the school if the Higginses agreed to pay for boarding until the school term was over. This gave them three months to raise enough money to start building facilities on the property they had purchased outside of Lira.

The Higginses had limited resources, but were able to raise enough money, along with some child sponsorships, to build a few basic African-style homes to house the children and to help clothe and feed them. They were able to obtain more mats for the children as well as funds for food.

But there was much more needed to house the many orphans. When Bob Pagett heard about the situation, he had discussions with the Higginses and went to investigate what they now call the Otino-Waa Orphan Village.

Later, Bob took Jim Sankey and Joe Coffey to Uganda, along with several other friends invited by Jim Sankey. After visiting AOET, they went to Otino-Waa and, seeing the work there, ended up donating a significant amount of money for child support. When Bob came home, he raised additional moneys to build more homes. Bob Pagett also convinced others to go with him to build homes at Otino-Waa—people like Rob Stuart, who built two homes in honor of his two deceased sons. Rob said that was such a healing time to be able to build homes for orphans and to see the life of his sons perpetuated through that.

Today, Otino-Waa continues to house, feed, and help educate hundreds of children who have parents at these homes. "These orphan children now have a better sense of family as parents and children live together, cook and eat meals together," Bob Higgins said.

Many of these children are now raised and some have gone on to further their education, becoming nurses, teachers, lawyers, and many others who have become good parents and productive citizens of Uganda. Some of them have now come back to Otino-Waa and are working and supervising the ongoing ministry there. In the recent pandemic crisis, many of the older children were sent back to their villages to shelter in place. Word was just received that they are helping to teach other younger children in the village and are helping lift the spirits of everyone there. So empowering others is a gift that keeps giving.

Bob and Carol said, "We're just tremendously grateful for Bob and Char. We could not have brought in resources that they were able to bring. Their networking abilities were the key to helping us do what has been done."

One Project Begets Another

Help others achieve their dreams and you will achieve yours.

—Les Brown[59]

Often, Assist International has found that one project leads to another promising project somewhere nearby. This happened in Romania and is also happening in Uganda. There is no shortage of desperate needs in the places where God puts you, such as what has happened for Assist in both Eastern Europe and Africa, where much of the work of A.I. has been accomplished.

Sister Rosemary's Story[60]

I sought the Lord, and he answered me; he delivered me from all my fears.

Those who look to him are radiant; their faces are never covered with shame. (Ps. 34:4–5)

"In 2014 I became aware of a nun named Sister Rosemary," Bob said. "I'd heard of her from a friend, John Bongiorno, president of WorldServe, who was in contact with a group that was helping Sister Rosemary. From what he shared with me, I decided that on my next trip to visit Sam Tushabe at AOET in Uganda I needed to visit Sister Rosemary."

Sister Rosemary was one of nine children born in her family. From the beginning she was a dynamo in energy, in happiness, and in caring for others. Everyone in her family knew that she was special. Everyone in her village knew that from her youth, God had given her a compassionate heart to help others.

Even as a child, she would spend hours in church in prayer, and she began to feel that God wanted her to be a nun. When she was fifteen years old, she went to a convent and shared that she wanted to become a nun. Because she was tall and vivacious, and in the view of the Catholic nuns at the convent had a recognizable call of God on her life, no one asked her what her age was.

So, at the age of fifteen, she took a vow of poverty and celibacy and gave her life to care for the poor and needy. It was later they discovered she had taken the vow before she was of age. She laughed her contagious laugh and said, "Well, now that I have taken the vow of poverty, no one should keep me from fulfilling the vow that I have made before Almighty God."

After she spent time in training and learning the disciplines of being a nun, she was asked to serve in Gulu, the largest city in the extreme north of Uganda, a dangerous city being brutalized by the Lord's Resistance Army. She had come from that city and had fled because of the LRA but, because of her devotion to God and the respect she had of her superiors, she said she was willing to live her life for the Lord in Gulu.

Bob said, "Someone sent me a YouTube video of Sister Rosemary entitled, 'Sewing Hope,' and it broke my heart. That an evil army could capture innocent young girls and force them to join the Lord's Resistance Army was unthinkable." The video features three girls who were captured and forced to become the "wives" of their captors. To start with, the girls were ordered to kill at least five people, and some of them had to be members of their own family. Because these girls were so young and had never faced such things, out of fear of their own lives they had to do what the LRA said or die. When the girls were captured, they had to march to where the LRA was located.

One girl in the march tells a heart-wrenching story. She, and her little sister who was with her, came to a river they had to cross, but her little sister did not know how to swim. The LRA leader told her to put her sister on her back and swim across the river. She begged for help, knowing she was not a good swimmer. The leader gave her an option: either take your sister across the river or kill your sister right now. No other LRA soldier would help this desperate girl, and they laughed as she agonized over what to do. Finally, she decided to try to take her sister on her back, but as she reached the water level above her head, she could not support her sister above the water and turned back to the riverbank.

When some girls and their children were able to escape the grip of the LRA they tried to go back to their communities and discovered that their parents had been murdered. And others in the community would not accept them. "You are the wife of murderers, and your children are the children of murderers," some told them. It was a crushing blow to not be welcomed back, knowing that they were still being hunted by the LRA for desertion.

Thank God that there was a nun in Gulu who was willing to take the girls and their children in, to give them a hope and a future. Sister Rosemary showed them the love of God and taught them what Jesus had done on the cross. She let them know that God forgives their sin and remembers it no more. She encouraged everyone not to talk about the past. That past was now over.

When the girls heard that Sister Rosemary would take them in to help them and their children, many of these young women came with their children for help. They lost the opportunity of getting an education, so they did not know how to make the money to care for their children. Sister Rosemary's convent became a place of rescue. She taught them to sew uniforms for boys and girls going to school. They learned culinary skills, by which they made cakes and decorated them for birthday parties and other kinds of celebrations. They were able to make a living.

Some of the girls had been captive of the LRA for up to nine years. One girl was always a loner. She could not face looking at anyone, including Sister Rosemary, and never talked to anyone. One day Sister Rosemary took the girl aside and asked her to look at her, but the girl refused. Sister Rosemary said, "Is it because my face is so ugly that you cannot look at me?" Finally, the girl looked at her and began to tell Sister Rosemary of the nine years of being with the LRA. Sister Rosemary told her that God had forgiven her, and that she needed to look to the future and not to the past. She told her that when God forgives someone the sin is never again remembered. Sister Rosemary, by her love and care, was the face of Jesus to this girl and her life began to change.

The LRA would come into the city at night to capture girls and cause all kinds of havoc. At the convent in Gulu, Sister Rosemary would shut their doors at 5 p.m., and with the women and their children they would hide in the hiding places and hallways of the convent. The building was large and there were places to hide; she risked her life to spare the lives of the girls.

One time, there was a father who fought for his children and his wife and killed a couple of LRA soldiers; he was then killed. The LRA then were out to kill his wife. She ran to the convent to seek refuge and asked Sister Rosemary if she would take her in. At great risk, Sister Rosemary allowed her into the convent, and she hid under Sister Rosemary's bed. The LRA came and asked her if she was hiding anyone. They walked into her bedroom to look around. They were blinded to the fact that the lady was under Sister Rosemary's bed.

The sisters knew that they were not able to keep her there, so they dressed her as a nun and told her, "You cannot cry if we are stopped, or they will know you are not a nun." So, a group of nuns were put into the back of a small, covered truck with the girl who was also dressed as a nun. As the vehicle left Gulu, the truck was stopped by the LRA. They looked in the back of the truck and saw a group of nuns. They let them pass and she was able to go to a place of safety.

Bob says, "God used Sister Rosemary in an amazing way to rescue the young girls who were kidnapped by the Lord's Resistance Army in northern Uganda. She brought healing to young women and rescued many vulnerable children in the Atiak region of Uganda through her orphan village and school called Sewing Hope Children's Home.

"Because we were in Uganda to help Sam Tushabe in Jinja, Uganda, we made it a point to go meet Sister Rosemary in Atiak in the extreme north of Uganda, thirty kilometers from the South Sudan border. We saw with our own eyes the women and their children that they had taken in. They needed homes like the ones we had built in Romania where the girls could raise their children in a home where they could be given a hope and a future.

"When we returned home from Uganda, I talked to Jim Sankey and a pastor friend of his, Joe Coffey, from Hudson Chapel in Ohio and asked if they would go with me to meet Sister Rosemary in Gulu. Jim chartered a plane; he invited some of his friends, and off we flew from the East Coast of the United States to Uganda. The plane landed in Gulu where we were met by Sister Rosemary and taken to where she wanted a village in Atiak. Jim Sankey generously donated enough money to build a primary school and five orphan homes. Other resources came in as well, to where there was enough to build a village of ten homes with a gathering place in the middle of the circle of homes, where food is cooked and where everyone gathers to eat and fellowship with one another."

*   *   *

These individuals in Uganda—Sam Tushabe, Bob and Carol Higgins, and Sister Rosemary—are examples of extraordinary people whose paths crossed with Bob and Charlene as people trying to help other people. They inspire us to know that we too can come alongside others who are getting the job done—sometimes in the most unlikely places.

The paradox about giving to those in need is realizing how much we learn from them, how much we receive from them. Some of us have more resources than others, but we all have something. People like a dear blind woman living on $700 per month who faithfully gives $30 a month to support orphan children. Or an elderly widow who sews baby bundles to give to poor mothers for their newborn babies, and also contributes from her resources to drill freshwater wells in Africa. We all can come alongside someone else and give a hand to empower others.

And a unique dynamic happens when we give to those who are close to God's heart. James wrote, "Pure and undefiled religion before God and the Father is this: to visit orphans and widows in their trouble, and to keep oneself unspotted from the world" (James 1:27, NKJV). James continued, "Has not God chosen the poor of this world to be rich in faith and heirs of the kingdom which He promised to those who love Him?" (James 2:5, NKJV).

There are no great people in this world, only great challenges which ordinary people rise to meet.

—**William Frederick Halsey, Jr.**[61]

CHAPTER TEN

THE POWER OF EXCELLENCE

We are what we repeatedly do. Excellence,
then, is not an act, but a habit.

–Aristotle

While Bob tends to "say yes, and then figure it out," both he and Charlene have made it their lifestyle to bring their best to every situation. Not in a legalistic, my-way or the-highway, but as a habit of doing things well. They have imprinted this quality into the work they have done through Assist International, as Bob insists that things be done right and with excellence.

Bob remembers, "When I was a boy, my twin sister and I had to help clean the house. And my mother insisted, 'When you sweep and mop the kitchen floor, be sure to get all the corners and under the edge of the cabinets. I want all the hidden places of the floor to be cleaned.' So, I learned by mopping the kitchen floor that details are important. And I've lived with that concept my whole life. I wash and vacuum my car the same way. I believe that if you're doing anything, do it right. And with the projects we do all over the world, part of it is being a witness for Christ. I think that every Christian if they're getting involved in something, they need to do it better than anybody else."

Charlene's father was a carpenter who insisted that his work be a work of excellence. When framing a house, he would not allow the walls to be even an eighth of an inch out of level. He always said, "If you allow a wall to be even slightly crooked or the framing studs to be out of line, all the rest of the work will also be out of line." Charlene said, "My dad built the house we live in forty-six years ago, located on a hillside, and it is still rock solid, even after going through the 6.9 Loma Prieta earthquake in 1989!"

A verse from Colossians affirms this powerful principle that is interwoven throughout Bob and Char's life: "Whatever you do, work at it with all your heart, as working for the Lord, not for human masters" (Col. 3:23).

Excellence: Attention to Detail

> *If a man is called to be a street sweeper, he should*
> *sweep streets even as Michelangelo painted, or*
> *Beethoven composed music, or Shakespeare wrote*
> *poetry. He should sweep streets so well that all the hosts*
> *of heaven and earth will pause to say, "Here lived a*
> *great street sweeper who did his job well."*

—Martin Luther King, Jr.[62]

The power of excellence is an amazing power that we often overlook. But regardless of what we do in life—whether it's parenting, teaching, or running a business or a profession—doing our best helps bring success. Its results come out of paying attention to the little things—the details, the follow-up. A good writer learns to edit and re-edit words so that they effectively convey meaning. Perhaps you know of an excellent teacher or speaker, and you admire the results you see. We admire a neighbor's beautiful yard, noting the care she gives her plants—and the results show it. Excellence may be in preparing the best sour cream chicken enchiladas and presenting it with fresh cilantro.

Excellence is a way of pursuing the best, not just a slap-dash acceptance of the mediocre. And let's face it: excellence means extra work and effort. But our efforts are rewarded if we keep at it. Behind the success lie hours of hard work and dedication. The apostle Paul wrote, "Let us not grow weary while doing good, for in due season we shall reap if we do not lose heart" (Gal. 6:9, NKJV).

Throughout their lives, Bob and Char have seen the benefits of pursuing excellence through the projects they have done with other partners, as they commit to complete projects that function properly and provide training for the local staff. They make sure installed equipment is functioning accurately and commit to making repairs or replacing faulty equipment at their expense if things go wrong. They see that things are done *right*. Excellence is worth it.

Unfortunately, there are reports where used medical equipment was sent out to various parts of the world that is now in a junk pile. In an article titled "Rage against the Busted Medical Machines," Nahid Bhadelia said:

> When medical equipment breaks down in the developing world, it often stays broken. There are usually few supply chains to get replacement parts, and local technical expertise is sparse. Even when

the machinery isn't broken, it may not be useful. In some cases, the donated machines need voltage that is incompatible with the electrical supply (if it's available and consistent) in the target country. Or the machine itself may work but the supplies needed to make it usable may have run out. I have also noticed that there is often a mismatch between the equipment donated and the capacity of the health-care facility to actually use the machine. What good is a ventilator when you donate it to a facility that has no health care workers with training to use it or steady electricity to keep operating it?[63]

It is estimated that between 40–70 percent of medical equipment in some countries is donated or funded through foreign sources, but that only 10–30 percent of the donations are ever put into operation. "There is no question that you can donate effectively," said Robert Malkin, a professor of the practice of bio-medical engineering at Duke University but added that it takes a lot of effort to make sure everything is done right. "There is a great risk for every medical device donation that it's going to hurt the recipient."[64]

Bob tells the story of a medical project they did in Timiso-ara, Romania: "When we arrived, we noticed that the doctors and nurses we spoke to were skeptical of what we planned to do. They took us on a tour of the hospital and showed us a room stacked with a variety of donated medical equipment that did not work. It was either broken or missing parts which made these various machines unusable. One was an Xray machine that had been donated that was sent to them without an Xray tube, which is the most expensive part to replace. We saw a junk heap of discarded medical equipment in many of the places where we went to do medical projects."

Excellence is not a short cut. The famed coach John Wooden asked, "If you don't have time to do it right, when will you have time to do it again?" Ultimately, doing things the right way builds integrity and brings success.

Bob said, "We make sure we send out all the needed accessories, plus qualified biomed engineers not only to install the equipment, but to train local biomed engineers how to operate it. We also send doctors and nurses that train all the local staff on steps needed to maximize the use of the machines. We then follow up later to make sure the equipment continues to work and send out qualified repair people, along with the parts needed, if something breaks down."

Excellence May Mean Flexibility

Excellence is not an exception; it is a prevailing attitude.

—Colin Powell[65]

Bob and Char have learned over the years that one of the biggest challenges faced is the fluid relationship between all the various aspects of successful health care. Health system strengthening is not always a linear problem to solve. You can't just say step one is providing equipment or clean water. But to ensure sustainability, you must make sure biomeds are trained to repair equipment, and that technicians know how to maintain the water filtration system. You must couple things like equipment donations with service contracts and biomedical engineering training.

Assist International has developed a thorough process to determine a project's viability before it's started.

Firsthand Observations

Aaron Fruh, president of Israel Team Advocates International, was involved in a hospital project in Israel and writes his observations of how the power of excellence shaped the project:

What impressed me most was the methodology behind the success of the project. I'm sure there are many more criteria involved in an Assist International project but in my experience in the Ma'ayanei Ha Yeshua project there were five impressive steps after saying "Yes" to do the project in Israel:

1. **Fact Finding**

   The first phase in Assist International's methodology was the fact-finding mission. Nearly one year prior to the installation of the equipment at Ma'ayanei Ha Yeshua Hospital, I traveled to Israel with Bob Pagett, Ralph Sudfeld, and Jim Stunkel to glean information. We visited five hospitals across Israel, meeting with doctors and hospital administrators in search of the best recipient.

2. **Selection**

   The fact-finding team was drawn to Ma'ayanei Ha Yeshua because of its extreme need of the equipment Assist International could provide. In a meeting with the dedicated doctors and administrators of Ma'ayanei Ha Yeshua I vividly remember the hospital's chief administrator asking Bob, "Why are you doing this?" To which Bob replied, "To fulfill our mission of matching resources with the great needs of the world." I remember thinking at that moment, *That's the central yet simple dynamic to Assist International's success.* The Assist International leadership ended up choosing Ma'ayanei Ha Yeshua for that key reason—their desperate need. The second reason, which I learned had become a highly important component of Assist's methodology, was the recipient's ability to facilitate the long-term management and maintenance of the new technology.

3. Story

During the next year Assist International found partners and sponsors for the Ma'ayanei Ha Yeshua post-operation department and discovered a story. Assist learned that Daniel Pearl, the *Wall Street Journal* reporter who was beheaded by Al-Qaeda terrorists in Pakistan in 2002, had roots in Bnei Brak, Israel. Daniel's last words before being murdered were, "My father is Jewish, my mother is Jewish, I am Jewish. Back in the town of Bnei Brak, there is a street named after my great-grandfather Chaim Pearl, who is one of the founders of the town." Assist also learned Daniel's grandmother still lived in Bnei Barak and that his father, Judah Pearl—a professor at UCLA—had been brought up there. The Ma'ayanei Ha Yeshua Hospital project was called the Daniel Pearl Project, in honor of Daniel Pearl. Over the years I have been impressed that Assist International's projects always are connected to a heartfelt story of hope that is born out of great need and loss. The stories add voice and meaning to the projects. This I believe is one of the unique abilities of Assist International—the gift of telling passionate stories about the extreme needs around the world by emphasizing the "human" side of humanitarian projects which are always logistically and technologically challenging endeavors.

4. Installation

At this point in the project, Assist had surveyed five hospitals in Israel, selected a recipient that had a desperate need and could manage the new equipment long-term, and communicated the story of need to help a small hospital in an impoverished town in Israel during the time of the Intifada when Jews in Israel were being murdered in suicide bombings. The next step was to send a team to Israel to install the medical equipment. A wing of Ma'ayanei Ha Yeshua Hospital had been remodeled in anticipation of the ten-bed post-operation department, a shipping container arrived in Bnei Brak from the Assist International warehouse in California and an Assist International technical team was now in Israel to wire the new space for the advanced equipment.

5. Dedication

When the installation was complete, I traveled to Israel with Bob and Char Pagett and a group of Assist International partners who had invested in the Daniel Pearl Project. Our purpose was to dedicate the new post-operation department with central monitoring station at Ma'ayanei Ha Yeshua Hospital in Bnei Brak. Daniel Pearl's father, Dr. Judah Pearl, flew in from UCLA for the special event.

As we flew back to the States, I reflected on the five elements that made the Daniel Pearl Project a success: fact-finding, selection, story, installation, and dedication. I concluded that it was an honor and privilege for me to be a part of such a meaningful journey. I also realized this was a very professional approach to making a project successful and it gave me a deep appreciation for all the steps that go into Assist International's central, yet simple mission of matching resources with the world's needs.

Financial Excellence

> *It takes twenty years to build a reputation and five minutes to ruin it. If you think about that, you'll do things differently.*
>
> **—Warren Buffett**[66]

One of the hallmarks of Assist International is their financial accountability. Early on, Bob told his board of directors that his goal was to keep the overhead costs of Assist International at a minimum. So, the board set up various policies to create a system that allowed most donated moneys to go to the projects, rather than the overhead.

Charity Navigator rates Assist International as a four-star nonprofit organization, their highest rating. Assist International's website states, "Ninety-five percent of every donation goes directly into our programs that address the needs of the world's vulnerable people."

Clayton Christiansen, the world-renowned innovation expert said, "Most of us think that the important ethical decisions in our lives will be delivered with a blinking red neon sign: CAUTION: IMPORTANT DECISION AHEAD. Never mind how busy we are or what the consequence might be. Almost everyone is confident that in those moments of truth, he or she will do the right thing. After all, how many people do you know who believe they do not have integrity?

"The problem is," Christensen said, "life seldom works that way. It comes with no warning signs. Instead, most of us will face a series of small, everyday decisions that rarely seem like they have high stakes attached. But over time they can play out far more dramatically."[67]

There are many references in the Bible about how the overwhelming desire to obtain wealth in a capitalistic society like the one we live in can have a profound effect on how we make important decisions about the money that runs through our hands—even when that money may not belong to us or may not be intended for our personal use.

Stories about the most vulnerable people tend to pull on the heartstrings and people want to give, believing that their donations will help the poor. How essential it is to maintain trust with donors, to protect the recipients of the funds, often given sacrificially. To receive funds from donors is a trust not to be held lightly. Financial integrity is a high form of excellence.

I (Bill) recall a time while on the board of directors of Assist International when we did a project with a foundation partner that gave the fund for the project based on a budget we provided. When the project was completed, it was finished more efficiently and with less money than projected. Once the foundation was informed of this, they redirected the excess funds for added program impact.

Colin Powell said, "If you are going to achieve excellence in big things, you develop the habit in little matters. Excellence is not an exception, it's a prevailing attitude."[68]

Bob said, "In the book of Wisdom it says, 'The integrity of the upright will guide them, But the falseness of the treacherous destroy them' (Prov. 11:3). We have always tried to live by a high standard of integrity, even when it might cost us more than it should."

Rick Ezell said, "Integrity is not reputation—others' opinion of us. Integrity is not success—our accomplishments. Integrity embodies the sum-total of our being and our actions. Integrity is not something we have, but something we are."[69] This means we are the same people in private as we are in public. It means we face challenges straight up, take responsibility for mistakes, take care in how we treat others, be honest with how we handle finances, give credit to those who deserve it, and refuse to compromise our principles and values.

Paula Downing along with her husband Sam, the CEO of Salinas Valley Memorial Healthcare System, went on numerous trips with Assist International to various parts of the world. She said, "There are very few people you can say that actually walk the talk. Bob and Char are in that group. They are an inspiration and amazing examples of how God works in your life." One thing we heard over and over as we talked to those who have worked with Bob and Char were words like "authentic," "genuine," "the real deal."

Ligia Dugulescu, executive director of JHOR in Romania, said, "Bob and Char never come with an attitude of superiority but with a humble, learning spirit; they respect every culture, every tradition, every person! They are unifying all people, loving all people, speaking, and fighting for the most vulnerable, for human dignity and biblical values. They build bridges between people of different religious beliefs, social status, education levels. They look at all the beautiful things that people have inside, never trying to change anybody, but presenting the One who can change anyone."

Having an authentic character has been a critical ingredient in Bob and Char's success in building Assist International into what it is today. This is something that is required of anyone who is going to not only succeed in the short run but succeed in keeping your calling intact for your entire life.

Excellence Leads to Integrity

*All labor that uplifts humanity has dignity and impor-
tance and should be undertaken with painstaking
excellence.*

—Martin Luther King, Jr.[70]

Rick Ezell said, "Integrity is not only about authenticity and truth-
telling; it is also about convictions. A person of integrity stands for
what is right. One cannot be a person of integrity without deep
convictions. They know what they believe and why. Convictions
are not forced on an individual; they are beliefs and actions of
choice."[71]

Integrity means being true to one's principles. One potential partner contemplating working with Assist International
was reluctant to support a project for a Catholic hospital in
Africa because of a policy to maintain their own "nonsectarian" status. Bob responded that Assist International works in all
cultures and with people of all different religious and political
groups. He explained that their definition of "nonsectarian" was
their willingness to work with all groups if it fit their mission
of helping the most vulnerable. He suggested to this partner
that if they were indeed "nonsectarian," yet they would support any hospital *except* a faith-based hospital (that cares for
all people without culture or religious barriers), the funder was
in fact adopting a specific sectarian bias. Bob said, "We do not
discriminate." The funder suddenly realized the contradiction
of their own philosophy and changed his position. And they
funded the project.

As we were writing this book, we were stuck at home (with
millions of others!) watching on television as the COVID-19

virus unfolded. We were sad to hear about a man who stole thousands of N-95 masks that were critical to the health care workers on the front lines of the battle. He was caught because he tried to resell them for exorbitant prices. Some may think they can get an advantage without being a person of integrity. But in the long run, this will always be a recipe for failure. "Whoever walks in integrity walks securely, but whoever takes crooked paths will be found out" (Prov. 10:9). However, the stories of heroes on the front lines of the fight against the pandemic inspire us to see how sacrifice and working hard to slow the spread of the virus and find a vaccine is bringing hope to many.

The world today is going at a breakneck speed. Internet and iPhones have not only changed how we do life but have also allowed us to work from behind the screens of our devices, often never looking at others eye to eye. This has caused all types of scams, computer viruses, online theft, and deceptions of different types where people congregate online. In many ways it is a "photo-op" world. It becomes increasingly difficult to know if the person you "friend" might really be the person in their profile, if the "news" or "tweet" you read is truthful, or even if the photos you see are doctored. It is essential more than ever to become people of truth, of our word. People of excellence.

Excellence: Pushing Through—No Matter What!

Don't give up. Normally it is the last key on the ring which opens the door.

—Paulo Coelho[72]

Sometimes excellence means not giving up. It may mean being creative and determined to see something through, even though the process seemed daunting. pushing through to get the job done and done well.

I (Nancie) saw the quality of persistence in Char last summer. Bob and Char were in Oregon to celebrate her eightieth birthday. While it's true that Bob doesn't have the word "quit" in him, neither does Char.

Bill and I planned to hike Iron Mountain in the Cascade Mountain range near our home last July—just when the wildflowers are at their peak. I'd done the hike several times with friends, and longed for Bill to see it, too. He said, "Okay, let's go—and invite Bob and Char and Jim and Carol along, too." While it is a beautiful hike, it's admittedly difficult. Not for the faint of heart.

So, the six of us (the three siblings plus spouses) set out on a sunny, sweet summer day with our hiking sticks, packed lunches, and lots of laughter and joking. I was a little nervous, being the tour guide, as I'd often hiked it. It did turn out to be a hard hike as we all began to experience the rocky, slippery, and steep path in some places. In the difficult places, we held our breath (and each other). But neither Bob nor Char would quit until we reached the top. None of us gave up and we made it to the lookout tower.

In hindsight, we probably should not have done it. But oh! The flowers were exquisite. After we (finally) got back to the car, we were all relieved to still be in one piece. And I have not heard the end of leading that hiking adventure! But I thought, sometimes life is like that mountain hike. And seeing Char get to the top on her eightieth birthday with Bob close behind was a triumph (who does that, anyway, on one's eightieth birthday?)!

Mountaintop experiences on a sunny sweet day are wonderful, especially when we get to the top. But it takes persistence to get there. Certain, rare times of life can be like the sun-drenched meadow, and we would like to stay there always. But truthfully, the moments of triumph are rare. Much of life is like climbing the mountain—exhausting, uncertain, painful, tedious. It takes commitment to push through, especially when there are lofty goals to reach.

Living a life of excellence can be hard, and many voices today would tell us that nobody should have to work this hard, that nothing is worth this kind of pain. But the battle is won not so much in blinding moments of truth as it is in hanging in there when the going is tough. Eyes on the goal. Excellence means to endure the difficult before the success.

Char has not stopped her pursuit of excellence in life. And neither has Bob. It's said, "You are what you do, not what you say you'll do." Bob and Char have lived that attitude of excellence with their relationships, family, and life's work.

> *Character consists of what you do on the third and fourth tries.*
>
> **—James Michener**[73]

Why is excellence important to us today?

Excellence clarifies our convictions. Francis Kelley wrote, "Convictions are the mainsprings of action, the driving powers of life. What a man lives are his convictions." [74] Martin Luther King, Jr. often told his children, "If a man has nothing that is worth dying for, then he is not fit to live."[75]

Excellence strengthens our influence. Excellence differs from a perfectionistic attitude, as it inspires, not intimidates. It's being the best version of yourself and sets a standard for others to model and a way to attain worthy goals. Jim Sankey, who has done several projects related to orphan children in partnership with Assist International, said of Bob Pagett, "I met Bob approximately twenty-five years ago when we went to Romania together. I have had a heart for orphaned children, and I was given Bob's name as a person who was involved in orphanages. I have been privileged to help support these organizations Bob has been working with. Bob has been an amazing role model for me, and I am sure many others, based on his total commitment to help those less fortunate. There is really no one I have ever admired more than Bob."

True excellence honors God. Excellence is an intentional direction, a pursuit. In the book of Daniel, we read the story of how Daniel became a man with a "spirit of excellence" and rose to great influence in a foreign land. The definition of "excellence" means something valuable; distinguished; honorable. Excellence is a comprehensive habit that make our lives honorable, with beautiful and life-nourishing results.

The secret of joy in work is contained in one word—
excellence. To know how to do something
well is to enjoy it.

—Pearl Buck[76]

CHAPTER ELEVEN

PASSING ON THE PASSION

Everyone leaves a legacy, whether they want to or not.
The question is, "What kind of legacy will you leave?"

—Dillon Burroughs[77]

Bob and Charlene Pagett delight in their family—in every single one of them. At the time of this writing there are two daughters; two sons-in-law; seven grandsons; two granddaughters; four granddaughters-in law; and two great-grandsons. Bob and Char's passion for their humanitarian work made it natural for them to include their family. And this passion of theirs has influenced their children and grandchildren too, as they have caught the vision to engage their own generation in various ways.

Jesus told his disciples, "he who believes in Me, the works that I do he will do also; and greater works than these he will do, because I go to My Father" (John 14:12, NKJV). Since Jesus is the Son of God, we can't help but wonder how it could be possible for any of us to do greater works than Jesus. Perhaps it refers to scope. Jesus never traveled physically more than sixty miles from where he was born; and yet each succeeding generation has carried his message of love and redemption around the world.

Compassion for the one—to give a "cup of cold water in Jesus's name"—has a way of multiplying. And so, it seems that Bob and Char's vision of reaching the vulnerable is meeting even more needs now as the scope of Assist continues around the world—not only through their own children, but in many other younger people they have mentored and influenced over the years. Bob and Charlene spent many years as youth directors and their faith and passion were contagious to the generation that followed them.

A living legacy does not mean being perfect; it means being real. It means relying upon God's strength in our weakness as we aim to do God's work. It is not so much a matter of *telling* the next generation what their values should be but *living* those values no matter what life throws at us. It is lived out in daily moments. Chris Marlow wrote, "How we respond to moments of interruption determines who we become and how we spend our lives. But you can never fully live in your calling without going through struggle, fear, and failure. Our decisions in those moments determine the legacy we will leave."[78]

The best values and principles are caught, not taught. For Bob and Char, this meant not only sharing their family traditions and faith values but their vision. They shared their vision to help vulnerable people not only with younger people in their circle of influence but with their own family. It just came out of who they were. And that is true of all of us. Tavis Smiley wrote, "The choices we make about the lives we live determine the kind of legacies we leave."[79]

Challenging the next generation is action oriented. Dr. R. Kelly Crace wrote, "Passing on a legacy means the way we live our lives in front of our children and grandchildren, allowing them to see what is important to us, what actions we take, what principles we hold and refuse to compromise, what core values we would be willing to die for, what spiritual truths we live by every day."[80]

What We Do Makes a Difference

Carve your name on hearts, not tombstones. A legacy is etched into the minds of others and the stories they share about you.

—Shannon Alder[81]

One highlight for Bob and Char has been a tradition of taking each grandchild (individually) with them on an overseas trip. "I'm sure every grandparent has a special relationship with their grandchildren," Bob said. "We remember every stage of their growth." Bob and Char decided that they would take each grandchild on a trip when they reached the age of about thirteen. For every grandchild, their "thirteen-year-old trip" impacted their lives. Some have gone on to join the work of Assist International, others volunteer or donate occasionally, but all have a lasting impact from the opportunity to travel the world with their grandparents.

We asked Bob and Char's grandchildren—now young adults—how their "thirteen-year-old-trip" affected them, and below you will see their similar, but profoundly personal reflections:

"I was impacted by being able to engage interculturally, to hear and tell stories and to partner with communities quite different from my own. It instilled in me a deep sense of curiosity and compassion. My desire to be engaged and serve in things bigger than myself," said one.

"Watching the relief on the faces of the nurses and doctors when they saw medical equipment that they desperately needed being installed made a huge impression on me. I realize as the years go by, how that first trip changed my perspective on how I want to engage in my community and in the world. My grandparents are living examples of taking risks, trusting the Lord, and showing up as agents of change and hope," said another.

Some of us may not be able to take our children or grandchildren on overseas trips, but all of us can be "living examples. . . trusting God. . . showing up as agents of change and hope" wherever we are in life.

But it is more than just the mission trips that embedded Bob and Char's values into their family legacy. It has been lives continuously lived for a cause, lived with principle and integrity. And it is not unique to the Pagett family. While you may not have the same calling as Bob and Char, each day you are passing on values to your family and to those around you that are in your sphere of influence.

What would cause me (Nancie)—an adult with a senior citizen discount card—to go back into the store just this morning to let the clerk know she had forgotten to charge me for a blouse? It was my father's example of honesty and sterling integrity that he, a wheat farmer in Montana, set for me and my siblings years ago. Who we are influences the younger ones watching how we live. A living legacy has staying power.

Another grandchild said, "Before I went to Uganda with my grandparents at fourteen, I had no idea what to expect. To say the trip was eye-opening is an understatement. But one of the most rewarding parts of going on the trip is looking back on it many years removed. Being able to 'pop the bubble' of my life at such a young and impressionable age impacted my worldview. Realizing at fourteen that the world was so much bigger than the little community I grew up in gave me a profound new perspective on the important issues in life. It motivated me to work hard and take advantage of my opportunities while also keeping in mind the needs around the world. So, as I have been able to accomplish some career goals, I've always tried to make it a point to give back to those without the opportunities I've been given."

Another grandchild: "The trip opened my eyes to the idea that the American way of living isn't the only way. I didn't realize it until much later, but it also gave me a much broader perspective of how people from different backgrounds think, and as a result has allowed me to make connections with many people who I otherwise may not have connected with."

And another: "My first trip with Assist International came after growing up with the organization, as it was started about when I was born. This meant I had heard stories, watched my parents and grandparents travel, and give a lot to build Assist International. For my thirteenth birthday trip, I went to Rwanda and got to experience a medical mission trip firsthand. The trip was incredible— experiencing life in Rwanda, traveling with just my grandparents, and getting exposure to such a different culture. That trip was the first of multiple trips over the next five years and shaped my worldview. It gave me exposure to people, cultures, and faith that looked different than mine, and helped me see the value in all people having their needs met. My grandparents have some of the best hearts of anyone I know, and I am honored to know them and do life with them, even more so to know the work they've contributed to over the past thirty years."

Stories can have a profound impact. Each of us have unique stories about our childhood, about how we met our spouse, about what helped to shape us as young people, and about our own parents and earlier generations and what they were all about. Even the painful, difficult parts of our heritage and our own lives are instructive to us. We can learn from those stories what is most important. And then we can pass those stories and experiences along to our own children and grandchildren.

Sharing a legacy is a natural thing. It does not mean developing some sort of curriculum or course about what's important. It's living it—and simply bringing our children and grandchildren into our own experience. It means to share our lived experiences. One grandchild said, "My grandparents took me on my first real adventure, they showed me how beautiful people's stories are. I've since devoted my life to telling stories like that, and my thirteen-year-old trip serves as the spark to the inspiration."

Another grandchild said, "My involvement with Assist has really opened my eyes to how great we have it in life, even when we may not feel like it in the moment. It's also helped me to see how important it is that those of us who can help others need to prioritize it in our lives. It reminds me of the Great Commission, and while I may not be explicitly preaching the gospel while I am working in these hospitals, hopefully they are seeing God's love through the actions that I am taking.

"Keep in mind that almost everyone in the US, still has it better than most people around the world, and we can all do our part to make things better. For some of us that's donating time or money out of an abundance that we have; for others it might be as simple as taking out the trash or shoveling a sidewalk for your elderly neighbor."

Char tells a story about a trip with her granddaughter Sarah, and how intertwined life can be: "We were able to return to Razlo-Bansko, Bulgaria to do another smaller project. We had just completed a project in Cluj and took our granddaughter Sarah with us for these projects. On this trip with Sarah, our ICU nurse trainer was Betty Earle. Betty has been on twenty trips with Assist International and what made this one so special was that we met Betty while in the cafeteria of the Modesto Memorial Hospital about thirteen years previous, when Sarah was born.

"We were at the hospital because newborn Sarah had experienced some medical challenge and was in intensive care. Betty was the neonatal ICU nurse in charge of Sarah's care. While having coffee, Betty asked what Bob and I did, so we started talking about Assist International. She said she'd love to go volunteer on a project with us. That was the beginning of our relationship with Betty, who has been a fantastic trainer/teacher all over the world, and here she was on Sarah's first 'grandkid' trip with all of us!" Betty Earle's own passion to help train other nurses in other parts of the world is a vivid example of how vision gets communicated and passed on to others. "It only takes a spark to get a fire going," as the song says.

Clayton M. Christensen writes profoundly about passing on our values: "The end result of these good intentions for our children is that too few reach adulthood having been given the opportunity to shoulder onerous responsibility and solve complicated problems for themselves and for others. Self-esteem. . . the sense that 'I am not afraid to confront this problem and I think I can solve it'. . . doesn't come from abundant resources. Rather, self-esteem comes from achieving something important when it's hard to do."[82]

Bob recalls another trip with a grandchild, "The opportunity came to work on a medical project at the To Du Hospital, the largest children's hospital in Vietnam in Ho Chi Minh City, formerly Saigon. As with other of our grandchildren, my grandson rolled up his sleeves unpacking boxes, organizing medical equipment with the help of an expert and being busy to help in any way he could."

From there they flew to Beijing, where they were welcomed by a representative of the Chinese Association for International Understanding for whom Assist International had already done several projects.

Daniel Scott said, "Your children are not your legacy. Your children may very well be your highest priority, the center of your universe, and perhaps you feel that everything you do is for them. . . Still, your children are *not* your legacy. *You* are your legacy, and the life you live, by choice or by happenstance, is the legacy you will ultimately leave behind."[83]

Creating Leaders

Leaders don't create followers; they create more leaders.

—Unknown

One of Bob and Charlene's grandsons, Chase Reynolds is a valuable part of the "on-the-ground team" that assists in projects in many countries. He tells of how his work has made an impact on his sense of compassion. "The work that Assist is doing really is making a difference for people. Often, working only on the medical programs and building project side of things, I am isolated from the people who are on the receiving end of our programs. I meet with doctors and nurses but don't interact with the patients. It's easy to get into a pattern of only hearing about the problems at the hospital, the equipment that doesn't work and the challenges of making sure our programs are running successfully, and forget that what we are doing is helping people that the hospital would not necessarily have been able to help six months earlier.

"But every so often, I see the tangible reasons why we do what we do. While visiting a hospital in Ethiopia we were working to put an anesthesia simulation center in for anesthesia students to train on before going into service, I saw a man in his midtwenties crying and being comforted by others. I asked the doctor we were with if he knew what was happening. He told me it was a case of maternal hemorrhage, and the mother would need emergency surgery to survive.

"In Ethiopia, and most of sub-Saharan Africa, there is a huge lack of anesthesia providers causing most rural hospitals to have to use nurse anesthesia providers that do not have the same level of training and skill that we take for granted. It was very impactful to see a situation that I was on the ground working to improve play out in front of my eyes," Chase said. "While I do not know the outcome of this man's family, I do know our program is now up and running at that hospital and I hope that future cases like that will have a happy ending in part due to the work we've done there."

Chase is clearly a young man who has embraced all the values and many of the characteristics of his grandfather, Bob.

Clayton Christensen said, "The natural tendency of many parents is to focus entirely on building your child's resume: good grades, sports successes, and so on. It would be a mistake, however, to neglect the courses your children need to equip them for the future. Once you have that figured out, work backward: find the right experiences to help them build the skills they'll need to succeed. It's one of the greatest gifts you can give them."[84]

Another grandson, Matt told me this story about his grandfather, Bob: "During the preliminary planning visit to Cuba, Bob met a guitarist at a downtown restaurant. They struck up a conversation, and eventually the guitarist asked Bob if he could bring him some new guitar strings when he visited again. A few months later, when I joined Bob and Char for the project, we went to that same downtown restaurant. Bob found the guitarist and gave him brand new guitar strings. I'll never forget the look of surprise on the guitarist's face. He couldn't believe that Bob remembered him. Bob and Char's legacy to me is how they always remember that each individual life matters and is worthy of love."

What Are We Leaving the Next Generation?

Let the world be a better place because you are here. Let unborn generations to come bless God because you once lived and poured out your potential to impact the world. Let them say, "We know a man who impacted the world positively and who through the use of his God-given potentials solved all the problems for which he was born." Let them say, "We know a woman who didn't deprive the world of her contributions to it."

—Clement Ogedegbe[85]

Bob and Char have set an inspiring example of intentionally investing in younger people. They have made a habit of helping others catch a vision of what's possible, not only in their grandchildren, but as former youth directors and while pastoring.

It is no secret or surprise there are many challenges ahead that our grandchildren and great-grandchildren will be left to tackle. It will take young people rising to face challenges in the next few decades. The best thing we can leave them is an example of our faith, that God will lead them and guide them to face the challenges of their own generation—if they will simply look to Him and ask for His direction.

Jerome C. Glenn of the Millennium Project in Washington, DC, said, "Humanity is facing major global challenges. . . including how to achieve sustainable development, guarantee access to clean drinking water, foster ethical market economies and fight new as well as re-emerging diseases. . . . [T]hese challenges cannot be addressed by any single government or institution acting alone. They require collaborative actions among governments, international organizations, universities, NGOs, and creative individuals. We need a serious focus on green growth, falling water tables, rising food/water/energy prices, population growth, resource depletion, climate change, terrorism, and changing disease patterns, otherwise the results may well be catastrophic."[86]

While statements like this sound overwhelming, when we put this into perspective of our day-to-day lives, it is as we teach our children the power of one and the values of reaching out to others—as the teachings of Jesus found in the New Testament point the way—that's when we achieve a measure of success.

Jesus said, "You will always have the poor among you, and you can help them whenever you want to. But you will not always have me" (Mark 14:7, NLT). Jesus was saying that when he would no longer be there, we would be the ones left to be the hands and feet of Jesus, reaching and going out to those in need. The things we do can make a profound difference in the lives of those we touch, even if it's only the lives of a few around us. Add all these "power of one" acts of kindness and help together, and we begin to see the masses being helped.

Jerome Glenn went on to say, "Fifty years ago, people argued that poverty elimination was an idealistic fantasy and a waste of money to try and eliminate; however, extreme poverty has fallen from 52 percent of the world in 1981 to about 20 percent in

2010. Extraordinary! Most of the world was in extreme poverty just thirty-one years ago and now less than 20 percent?! Pessimists are just not doing their homework. And today people argue about the best ways to achieve that goal, not whether or not it is worthwhile to try."[87]

Bob and Char Pagett: two ordinary people with extraordinary hearts, passing it on to the next generation, one person, one project at a time. It can happen for any of us if we have a dream and a passion to do whatever God is calling us to do. The possibilities are right in front of us. Ordinary people creating a small ripple that makes a difference in one life, one by one rippling around the world.

CHAPTER TWELVE

THE RIPPLE EFFECT

*Every time a person stands up for an idea, or acts to
improve the lot of others, or strikes out against injustice,
he sends forth a tiny ripple of hope, and crossing each
other from a million different centers of energy and
daring, those ripples build a current that can sweep
down the mightiest walls of oppression and resistance.*

—Robert F. Kennedy[88]

Every action creates a reaction. Every word we speak, every
action we make affects not only ourselves, but other people
as well, as our words and actions "ripple" out to others. Or maybe
what we *don't* say, or *don't* do. How essential it is then, to be
purposeful in our lives. Laurie Buchanan wrote, "Our personal
ripple effect is the power of one generating hope and change in
others for a better world. Like pebbles radiating across the surface
of a pond when a pebble is tossed in, kindness is powerful and has
far-reaching, positive ramifications that bring about a tremendous
sense of joy."[89]

Paul wrote to the Galatians, "A man reaps what he sows. . . . Let us not become weary in doing good, for at the proper time we will reap a harvest if we do not give up" (Gal. 6:7, 9). What a simple yet powerful principle. We see this principle played out in practical, emotional, spiritual, and physical ways. We see it in individuals and families; in communities; in churches; in businesses, and in nations. *What others do affect us. What we do affects others.* Sometimes we become aware of it, and often we are not.

We also see this principle in history, too. Bob Pagett has always loved history, fascinated by the stories of individuals and forces that shaped the destiny of people and nations for good or bad. Bob and Char began Assist International by being inspired by the results of the revolution in the Soviet Union and Eastern Europe and seeing the ripple effect of individuals standing up for freedom.

As young people, Bob and Charlene were influenced by their parents, their pastors, their mentors, and their experiences at Bethany Bible College and early ministry. The ripple effect in their lives continued as they became youth pastors, then directors of youth in the state of Oregon, sharing their vision of outreach. They often took teens with them on outreaches to places where people were underserved, and later as senior pastors in Santa Cruz, taking church members on multiple mission trips. The ripple effect from that is that many of these young people ended up going into missions or ministry work. The ripple effect continued as Bob and Char routinely invited leaders of Rotary and other groups, as well as pastors, to accompany them on humanitarian trips. The leaders and pastors in turn were inspired to do more outreach in their own circle of influence. And the ripple effect continues even now, changing lives and situations for the better as their children and grandchildren, as well as many other employees and volunteers, continue the mission of Assist International.

We must never underestimate how powerful our lives are, and that each of us have the capacity to affect our world in various ways for better or worse. Even the things we might consider small and inconsequential can create a ripple effect. A handwritten note of encouragement, or a simple text to someone expressing our gratitude, can be enormously life-giving. It can make the difference between hope and despair for someone.

Several years ago, Nancie and I wrote a book, *Lord, Bless My Child: Praying for the Character of God in Your Children*. At the time, our kids were small, and we had started expanding our prayers to be something more purposeful than just the rote prayers we prayed. It was helpful to us, so we decided to create a book to help other parents pray more effective prayers for their children. In each chapter we gave a principle we thought God wanted to develop in our children, along with some quotes, prayers, and a place for parents to journal their prayers.

When the book was released, little did we realize how impactful that book would be, as tens of thousands of copies have been released. We still hear from parents who tell us how it has impacted them and their children. One dad said he had prayed the prayers and journaled for all his kids and now needed new copies to pray for his grandkids. Another mom said that when her son graduated from high school, she handed him her copy of the book, with her journal entries, and said, "These are the prayers I have prayed for you over the years." It stays in print year after year, as it continues to inspire parents in their prayers for their children and grandchildren. We hope and pray that the "ripple effect" of sharing our own prayers for our own children will continue to have a positive impact on other parents and

184 LEAP of FAITH

grandparents whom we will never meet, who use this book to pray for their children.

Each one of us has a circle of influence. What we do and who we are matters to others, especially to younger people who are watching our lives. Take a moment to consider who has inspired you. Perhaps it is a teacher, a coach, a pastor, or a business leader. We have received much, and all of us can be intentional about giving back. It can start in the smallest of ways, just where we are.

Bob and Char could not have imagined that back in 1990, their passion to help vulnerable people would spread to countless thousands. Their passion to help the world's most vulnerable became contagious as others joined the cause, inspired by what they witnessed. Their work continues to ripple out and will no doubt outlive them. Living out one's calling with conviction and integrity will inspire others to do good as well.

Joe Hamilton, former Rotary Governor of District 5170, who has participated in many projects with Assist International, tells how this ripple affect happens:

"I encountered an amazing young woman in her midtwenties who was a nurse at Stanford Hospital and my wife was her patient. Her name is Obse (Ob-see) Lubo. When I met her in 2014, I discovered she was from Ethiopia. We discussed humanitarian efforts I had helped with in Djibouti with Rotary and Assist International and in Ghana with a polio national immunization day. I discovered that even at her young age she had organized and led several medical teams to her hometown of Nedjo, Ethiopia, to provide surgeries at a hospital with great needs. I also discovered she was a new Rotarian in Castro Valley Rotary, and I suggested her club develop a Rotary Global Grant to help meet the local medical needs.

"Based on her perception and information from the Nedjo Hospital, where needs were many, one of the most critical needs was oxygen. The hospital lacked an adequate supply due to the remoteness from an industrial-grade supplier in Addis Ababa, some fifteen hours each way over poor roads.

"She had no idea how to approach meeting the need. The individual and organization I knew who could give us advice was Bob Pagett. I knew that beyond any business possibilities, Bob would help. As usual, he gave of his time and helped Obse through understanding alternative ways to meet this need and personally brought the Assist International team's resources to subsequent meetings. He helped take Obse and a small Rotary Club of Castro Valley from a daunting, impossible attitude to something that could be done. For many years the motto of Rotary has been "Service above Self," and recently Rotary has adopted a new motto, "Service to Change Lives." In 2014, Bob and Joe convened with the Rotary Club of Castro Valley, and the members seized the vision for this project with a passion. The project committee was named 'Breathing for Life,' and with the partnership of Assist International a course was charted for the design of an oxygen production plant and all the necessary equipment to support a viable, sustainable medical oxygen production and delivery program based in Nedjo, Ethiopia. The budget for this program would require partnership funding by the Rotary International Foundation (RIF).

"By April of 2018, when half of the funding was raised, the RIF sent a representative to join the Assist International team in Ethiopia for the final project evaluation and approval. The project *was* approved, and work was begun. In August of 2020, six full years from the date of the first project committee meeting, the Nedjo Oxygen Plant was commissioned and began producing medical oxygen, fulfilling the vision for the largest Global Grant project in the history of Rotary District 5170.

"There is much magic in this story due to the many individual efforts, but it all started with the meeting with Obse Lubo, Bob Pagett, and me," Joe said. "Obse had a dream and knew of a need to end suffering a long way away, Bob Pagett helped breathe life into that dream."

Since Bob was a charter member of his local Rotary club, he started working on projects in his community with Rotary while he was pastor of a church. And when he launched into Assist International work, his passion rippled out to Rotary clubs across America and Rotary International, which became steady and crucial partners in accomplishing dozens of projects all over the world. People like Henning Sorknaes in Hungary, a Rotarian leader in Eastern Europe who helped raise grant moneys and influenced dozens of Rotarians in his part of the world to do incredible projects. Rotarians like Joe Hamilton, Jim Walker, Ron Sekkel, David Gallagher, Sue Marscellas, Russ Hobbs, Henning Sorknaes, and literally hundreds of Rotarians from many districts and various parts of the world have done life-changing projects in partnership with Assist International.

The Ripple Effect Can Change the World

> *I alone cannot change the world, but I can cast a*
> *stone across the waters to create many ripples.*

—Mother Teresa[90]

There are many causes that can become our passion, but we are not solitary islands who do these things alone. Whether you want to help feed the hungry, improve the environment, get involved in foster care, or simply help others in your church or neighborhood, it can start with you. And if it is successful, it will ripple out to others who are influenced by your passion.

Studies show there are many ways people influence others. Knowing Bob and Char for so long, my guess is that two of the ways they influence others are through these two actions:

- *Inspiration*: encouraging others toward their passion by communicating a sense of shared mission and exciting possibility, using inspirational appeals, stories, and metaphors to encourage a shared sense of purpose

- *Connection*: attempting to influence outcomes by uniting or connecting with others, relying on reciprocity, engaging superior support, consultation, building coalitions, and using personal relationships to get people to buy into their cause

Not only do Bob and Char bring others to *their* dream, but as we demonstrated already, they often come alongside someone else's dream, eventually inspiring them to launch out on their own. Andy Pierce is a classic example of someone who was inspired by Bob and Char to take his passion to the next level.

Project 41

Andy is a plumbing contractor in central California who went with Assist International to Haiti right after the January 2010 earthquake, where he saw the devastation, including the huge need for clean water. He noticed the need for people to have some way to pump water without electricity. He'd brought a small hand pump that would pump about five gallons per minute, but it was completely inadequate in relation to the need.

There are lots of backyard swimming pools where Andy lives, and a lot of his work as a plumber was replacing pool pumps with burned-out motors. When he came home from Haiti, he had a new vision about how to help struggling villages in Haiti. An idea emerged about these larger-capacity discarded pool pumps. While the motor was burned out, the actual pump was still in working condition. He thought about how it could be possible to separate the pump from the motor and then figure out a way to make it work. He ended up designing a contraption that used a bicycle to pump water. When trying it out, he realized it was quite efficient, by peddling the bike, to pump a substantial amount of water—fifty gallons a minute!

When he finished his first prototype pump, he called his good friend Jim Stunkel, who was a VP at Assist International and had been with Andy in Haiti. Andy wanted to send his pump to Haiti. He asked Jim if there was a forty-foot container going to Haiti that could include his bicycle pump.

What Andy didn't know was that Jim Stunkel, at that moment, was contemplating what he could do to fill a need for a remote health center in Uganda. "They didn't have running water and/or electricity. They needed some way to pump water into a gravity-feed water tower," Jim said. "So I was searching online, doing all sorts of research for a no-cost or minimum expense solution, when my phone rang. At that moment I had breathed a prayer, 'Lord, I need a solution, I don't know what to do about this.' I picked up the phone and Andy said, 'Hey man, how's it going?' I said, 'Andy, I'm totally frustrated. I got this small health center in a remote part of Uganda that needs to pump water into a gravity feed tower, and I got nothing.'"

Andy started to tell Jim about his new prototype bicycle pump he was hoping to send to Haiti. For a moment, it was like Andy was talking about Haiti and Jim was talking about Uganda and it did not register with either of them for the first moments of the conversation that Andy was telling Jim he had exactly what he needed. When Jim hears the words "water pump," "fifty-gallons a minute," "pumps uphill," suddenly Andy got Jim's attention.

"I'm like, 'Andy, I need a water pump in Uganda. Does this thing you've invented really work—I mean, *really work*?'" Andy assured Jim that he had tested it and yes, it really did work. Jim said, "Okay, come with me to Uganda and let's set it up there."

So, the Haiti pump was diverted to Uganda. Jim said, "Once it was up and running, I kid you not, everybody in the village came out and they were all amazed. Everyone wanted one for their crops and gardens, for their homes. It was an immediate success."

Jim, now completely sold on Andy's bicycle pump, came home from Uganda, and presented Andy's mission and invention to the Assist International board. There was immediate enthusiasm.

Bob called Andy and told him that the board wanted to adopt his project and give him support. What no one knew at the time was that due to the recession, Andy was out of work. Andy said, "When Bob called, I was relying on my wife's job to keep us afloat. My wife and I had gone 'all in' on this project, and I had started making more of these pumps on my own, but we were literally down to our last $3.50 when I received a call from Bob Pagett."

Andy named his new venture "P41." P41 stands for Project 41. The verse that inspired Andy was Isaiah 41:17–18 (NASB): "The afflicted and needy are seeking water, but there is none, and their tongue is parched with thirst. I, the Lord, will answer them Myself, as the God of Israel I will not forsake them. I will open rivers on the bare heights and springs in the midst of the valleys; I will make the wilderness a pool of water, and the dry land fountains of water."

Andy started enlisting other plumbers and pool repair companies to donate their burned-out pumps, even providing drop-off places where they could leave the pumps. Soon after this first project, Assist International and the Modesto, California Rotary Club got involved and Andy, along with about 150 of his P41 pumps and the plastic pipe needed, were sent to Uganda.

In parts of Africa like Uganda, due to weather cycles most farmers can only grow one crop a year during the rainy season; otherwise, there is no water to irrigate their small farms. But Andy knew that with his pump system, pipes could pump water to these small farms from available streams, ponds, and other water sources, allowing them to grow more than one crop per year.

In his research Andy discovered that he could show these small farmers how they could grow crops year around. "Statistics show that hunger and malnutrition claim more lives every year than AIDS, malaria, and tuberculosis combined," he said. His pumps provided more than double the output for a small farm—enough to not only feed the farmer's family year around but also to be able to sell part of his crop to earn income for other necessities.

Eventually, Assist International was able to help Andy launch out on his own, establishing P41.org. Andy calls himself "an accidental philanthropist." His organization today incorporates many corporate and foundation partnerships. "The inmates working at SPL have taken up our cause and are building our SafeTap filters for us," Andy said. "This amazing relationship allows us to make our systems available to other nonprofits or organizations interested in bringing clean water to the communities they are engaged in. Instead of giving up, these men in prison have chosen to give back. They are living examples that we can each do something."

You can see from this one story that the "ripple effect" is powerful. Not only did Andy find the inspiration and helpful resources from Assist International to get a start at his dream; but then his initial pumps brought help to poor struggling farmers, eventually bringing a more sophisticated clean water system to other parts of the world and eventually brought a new-found purpose to men in prison. It all started with a trip Andy took with Assist International to Haiti. It all began with noticing a need and taking action to do something about it.

Victoria Moran said, "The idea that everything is purposeful really changes the way you live. To think that everything that you do has a ripple effect, that every word that you speak, every action that you make affects other people and the planet."[91] Think of yourself as a small rock. When you cast yourself on the sea of life, the "ripple effect" takes place. Your actions, both good and bad, affect others around you, sometimes affecting people you have never met.

We Are Contagious

So, the question we must ask ourselves isn't, will I make a difference in the world? The real question is, what kind of difference will it be?

—Dennis Merritt Jones[92]

As we write, all of us are experiencing the effects of a global pandemic with the COVID-19 virus. It's said that it all started with one person and has now affected millions of people around the globe, bringing the entire world to its knees, costing thousands of lives and trillions of dollars. It was hard for most of us to imagine, prior to this pandemic, that a virus in one person could eventually shut down the economies of the entire world and kill hundreds of thousands of people.

What we are and what we do matters. Today's world is interconnected as never before. What you tweet or post on Facebook matters. What you may say in haste matters. How you treat those around you matters. All of us, one way or the other, make a difference, make ripples. You do matter and your dreams and ambitions matter.

Medical research teams invented COVID vaccines that will eventually impact millions of people they will never meet. Another writes a best-selling song or book that touches the lives of untold thousands. Athletic coaches and high school teachers will influence kids who will be inspired by them to go on to do great things for others. Others might make a worldwide impact, like Bob and Char Pagett, simply through living lives that matter.

Even if the ripple effect from your life only goes as far as the ones you love, the friends you share meals with, or the people you work with, your actions and words are creating a powerful ripple effect. It is not insignificant.

Our good friend Greg Salciccioli has a team of "life coaches" who work to help others go from where they are to where they want to be. One of his blogs on his Coachwell website is about how the ripple effect works even in the immediate family:

> If I come home from a stressful day and snap at my wife and kids, the negative ripple effect is released, and it changes the attitude of everyone in the home. My children anticipating my arrival are now offended and hurt which impacts their ability to complete their

homework, how they treat each other and even how they sleep. My wife is offended, and her mood shifts from soft and affectionate to cold and collected. The dinner table that usually contains lively interaction and sharing of each-others day is now quiet and somber. What a bummer! It could have been different.

What if I had stopped on the way home at a park and walked for fifteen minutes unloading the stress of my day? Praying as I walk, asking for divine assistance to refresh so I can bring strength rather than offend my family. I jump in the car and head home with a refreshed perspective and a renewed mission to "lift up" everyone at home. I come in the door, grab my bride, and give her a big kiss and hug—telling her how much I appreciate her and her beauty. I wrestle with the kids and pet the dog. Imagine now the "ripple effect" in my home![93]

No matter what life you choose, you are creating a ripple effect—for good, for mediocrity, or for evil. When Bob and Char first went to Romania three months after Ceausescu was dead, many couples shared with them about the communist policy under Ceausescu that encouraged having more children in order to build a future army; however, the result was that they were forced to put some of their children in state-run orphanages because they did not have enough money to feed their children and they could not keep their homes warm enough in the winter to keep their children due to laws that shut off the electricity at night. When things became desperate in Romania, they had heard that the state orphanages had food and warmth, so with many tears they gave some of their children over to the state-run orphanages. The evil "ripple effect" the communist regime had, rather than creating a vast number of strong youths whom Ceausescu envisioned for his future army, instead created one of the largest populations of poverty-stricken orphan children, many with criminal histories and sad outcomes, which continues to ripple through Romania to this day.

But on the good side. Think of the orphanages that Assist International has helped to bring into existence and continues to support in Romania and other parts of the world. Most of these children will grow up to become productive citizens, contributing to society and raising loving families which will continue to make a difference for good.

If you have taken anything to heart in this book, we hope you have seen that the "ripple effect" is a powerful force in every life, including yours. What started for Bob and Char as a closed door opened another door by taking a trip to Moscow, then grew from two people with a fax machine in a back bedroom into an organization that has literally touched tens of thousands of lives all over the world. C. S. Lewis said, "Miracles are a retelling in small letters of the very same story which is written across the whole world in letters too large for some to see."[94]

What is easy to forget is that big blessings start with one heart—one heart awakened to the needs of others, then recognizing one person, maybe right next to you, who is in need. This does not start with a big bang. It starts with opening our eyes. . . just noticing to see who is there, who possibly is hurting, who needs a friend, who can benefit from a simple gesture of kindness. It starts with a personal soul search to find our calling. A raging fire can start with only a spark. One stone tossed in the pond will create a ripple that reaches every inch of the surrounding shore.

You and I are not responsible for the whole world or for the insurmountable needs of the masses. But we are responsible for ourselves and how we manage our own lives. And that stewardship of self is not based on our race, religion, or color of our skin. It is not based on our social status, educational accomplishments, or economic status. It is based on the simple fact that we are alive and living somewhere with opportunities in front of us to use what gifts and resources we have to reach out to someone who needs exactly what we have to offer—even if all we have is sharing a meal or listening with empathy.

And yes, sometimes it may not be that easy. Most likely, when we really see what is in front of us. . . what needs our doing. . . it will cause us to step out of our comfort zone. Invariably it will challenge us to give of our time and resources. And it may even alter the entire course of our lives, as it did with Bob and Char. But in the end, when we take our own "leap of faith," it can become the most gratifying and meaningful thing we ever do. That is because it will not only change the people we choose to love, but it will put our own hearts in tune with God and bring us unspeakable joy.

The Story of Assist International Continues
As Ellen M. Perry said:

> Long before the written word, people told stories. Stories were part of the life fabric of the whole community, the glue that held a society together. They were as essential as food and shelter. One of the most basic and powerful of human experiences, stories are the most effective tool for communicating, because they enter our hearts by engaging our imagination. They are how we human

beings have passed on history and values, wisdom of the mind, and wisdom of the heart for thousands of years. Storytelling speaks to the human heart; it enriches the teller as well as the listener and we all have stories to tell; when we tell our stories, we are engaged in the act of discovering and creating meaning.[95]

Bob and Char have now passed the leadership reins to the younger generation. Ralph Sudfeld, their son-in-law, is now president of Assist International. Ralph said, "Going forward, Assist International will continue to build on the foundation created by Bob and Char over the past thirty years. We remain committed to meeting the needs and improving the lives of the most vulnerable people in the world, guided by the belief that every life is valuable. . . . We are committed to saving lives by strengthening health systems and bringing together the right partners so that we can achieve more than we could alone. We are committed to providing hope and a future to orphaned and abandoned children so that they can live full lives. We are committed to being missional, motivated by our faith to impact the world. And finally, we are committed to inspiring a new generation of people to witness firsthand the injustices in the world and challenging them to do something about it."

While no one can predict the future of Assist International, neither can anyone foresee the massive challenges, twists, and turns the world will face. The COVID-19 pandemic we are currently living through is testament to this. And, Assist International has been thrust into the middle of solving the problem of "access to medical oxygen" as a primary treatment for patients who have contracted COVID-19. Assist International is playing a significant role alongside the many outstanding international organizations and agencies that are working together to save lives of those impacted by the global pandemic. And one thing that Bob and Char and all the others associated with Assist International can clearly see by simply glancing back at where they have been. . . is the guiding hand of Almighty God.

There will never be a shortage of vulnerable people in the world or challenges like the ones we now face. As long as there are people like Bob and Char Pagett who rise to accept the challenge, there is hope.

Bob and Char, through the experiences of their lives—their early upbringing in faith-filled homes, their call to missions, the tragic loss of their infant daughter, their pastoral ministries—were brought to a place of a higher calling. In their early fifties, they discovered their greatest calling. It involved three simple but basic elements, even when they were not fully aware of them:

- Two ordinary people who felt compelled to improve the lives of other people less fortunate than they, finding a way to take the wealth of the world and apply it to the needs of the most vulnerable

- Two ordinary people who would inspire others to join with them, never caring about who got credit for what would get done

- Two ordinary people who didn't just believe *in* God, but who dared to *believe God*

By following these principles of faith, they became two of the most *extraordinary* people on this planet, especially in the lives of everyone they touched.

A FINAL WORD FROM BOB
AND CHAR

As we reflect on the stories in this book and the experiences God has brought us through, we are amazed at how big God is and how much *He* cares about the details of our individual lives. Through the darkest time of our lives at the death of our daughter, Pamela Renee, and then after nearly six years of devastating lung illness for Char, we reflect on that time often and thank God for seeing us through. During the COVID-19 pandemic and prior to receiving our vaccinations, we were "sheltering in place" for more than a year. It was a time of reflection for us. We are usually so busy planning travel, working on projects, getting on airplanes, and being with people in other countries, which being in lockdown was like suddenly hitting a brick wall. Everything came to a screeching halt: cancelling travel, airline tickets, hotels, working to get our staff that was out of country home safely, figuring out how to successfully work from home remotely; cancelling our gala thirtieth event and all that involved—and yet we saw God helping us and seeing us through once again.

As you've read through these chapters of *Leap of Faith*, you have seen where we have lacked faith, where we have been at our wits' end, needing miracles from God; and yet the faithfulness of

God always was there to see us through a lifetime of challenges, victories, and our human weakness. We pray that you, the reader, will be able to put your trust in God through the difficult times and know that we are all just human beings whom God loves and is willing to help always. It is impossible to measure success against pain, hurt, and misery in the world, but if we can in some small way set the oppressed free, share food with the hungry, provide the poor with shelter, clothe the naked, and bring health to the sick, that is what we seek.

At this autumn time of our life, we know God is asking us to pray more, trust Him more, and not waver in our faith toward Him. The scripture that is impressed on our hearts is Micah 6:8: "What does the Lord require of you? To act justly and to love mercy and to walk humbly with your God."

ENDNOTES

Dedication

[1] "She Was an Angel" was written at the time of Pamela's homegoing in February 1971, by Bill Carmichael.

Chapter One: Two Extraordinary People

[2] Oswald Chambers, *My Utmost for His Highest,* quoted in Oswald Chambers, *The Best from All His Books;* Chosen and edited by Harry Verploegh; (Nashville, Tennessee, by Oliver-Nelson Books, a division of Thomas Nelson, Inc., 1989), 85

[3] Mitch Albom, *Tuesdays with Morrie* https://goodreads.com>quotes 37196 accessed 10-8-21

[4] Michel Quoist, quoted in *Westminster Collection of Christian Quotations,* ed. by Martin H. Manser, 2001; https://books.google.com

Chapter Two: How It All Began

[5] Phillip Brooks, *Treasury of the Christian Faith;* (New York: Association Press, 1949), 263

[6] J. R. Miller, quoted in Mrs. Charles E. Cowman, *Streams in the Desert* (Grand Rapids, MI: Zondervan, 1980), 79

[7] J. W. Follette, *Broken Bread* (Springfield, MO: Gospel Publishing House, 1957), 33

[8] Nettie McCormick, Christianity.com/church/church-history/timeline/1801-1900 Nettie McCormick, 11630439.html. accessed 10-8-21

[9] Philip Neri, quoted in *The Doubleday Christian Quotation Collection*, Hannah Ward and Jennifer Wilds, eds. (New York: Doubleday, 1998), 101.

Chapter Three: Closed Doors—Open Doors

[10] Madame Jeanne Guyon, *Spiritual Torrents* (Augusta, Maine: Christian Books, 1984).

[11] "Joel Osteen Quoted," QuoteFancy.com, https://quotefancy.com/quote/838789/Joel-Osteen-Nothing-in-life-has-happened-to-you-It-s-happened-for-you-Every.

[12] Garth Brooks, "Unanswered Prayers," https://www.songfacts.com/lyrics/garth-brooks/unanswered-prayers.

[13] Masha Hamilton, "Bible Is Real Page-Turner at Soviet Fair," *Los Angeles Times,* September 16, 1989.

[14] Oswald Chambers *So Send I You,* (Mishawaka, INL Better World Books, 1973), 17

[15] "Oprah Winfrey," Quote Master, https://www.quotemaster.org/qa8b97f9666143819fde20d44c7828772.

[16] Os Guinness, *The Call:* Finding and Fulfilling the Central Purpose of Your Life (Nashville: W Publishing Group, 1998), 6.

[17] Rick Warren, *The Purpose Driven Life* (Grand Rapids, MI: Zondervan, 2002), 243.

[18] Chambers, *My Utmost for His Highest,* September 1, https://utmost.org/classic/destiny-of-holiness-classic.

[19] Donald O. Clifton and Paula Nelson, *Soar with Your Strengths* (New York: Bantam Doubleday, 1992), 44.

[20] James Allen, *As A Man Thinketh;* (Old Tappan, New Jersey: Fleming H. Revell Co., 1980), 54

[21] Frederick Buechner, *Wishful Thinking: A Theological ABC;* https://www.good reads/com/quotes 140448; accessed 10-8-21

[22] Chambers, *My Utmost for His Highest,* February 21, https://utmost.org/classic/have-you-ever-been-carried-away-for-him-classic, 202

Chapter Four: Embracing the Challenge

[23] Drenda Keesee, *Shark Proof* (Redding, CA: New Type Publishing, 2019), SharkProof Quotes https://www.goodreads.com>work>69197758

[24] "John F. Kennedy > Quotable Quote," GoodReads, https://www.goodreads.com/quotes/1487-the-chinese-use-two-brush-strokes-to-write-the-word.

[25] "Israelmore Ayivor > Quotable Quote," GoodReads, https://www.goodreads.com/quotes/6799547-every-big-castle-was-once-started-with-a-single-block.

[26] Human Rights Watch Interview with Eduard Petrescu, National Officer UNAIDS, Bucharest, Feb. 6, 2006.

[27] Martin Luther King Jr., *Strength to Love* (1963; Minneapolis: Fortress, 1963), 26.

[28] Keesee, *Shark Proof,* https://www.goodreads.com>work>69197758, 6

Chapter Five: Taking Risks

[29] "Frank Scully > Quotable Quote," GoodReads, https://www.goodreads.com/quotes/31336-why-not-go-out-on-a-limb-isn-t-that-where.

[30] John Piper, "Safety Is a Myth" (podcast), Desiring God, January 23, 2013, https://www.desiringgod.org/interviews/safety-is-a-myth.

Chapter Six: Saying Yes to the Opportunity

[31] "Jonas Salk Quotes," BrainyQuote, https://www.brainyquote.com/quotes/jonas_salk_390974.

[32] "Albert Einstein Quotes," BrainyQuote, https://www.brainyquote.com/quotes/albert_einstein_106192.

[33] "Helmut Thielicke > Quotable Quote," GoodReads, https://www.goodreads.com/quotes/231482-tell-me-how-much-you-know-of-the-sufferings-of.

[34] "Mary Anne Radmacher > Quotes," GoodReads, https://www.goodreads.com/author/quotes/149829.Mary_Anne_Radmacher.

Chapter Seven: The Power of One

[35] "Edward Everett Hale > Quotes," GoodReads, https://www.goodreads.com/author/quotes/8183.Edward_Everett_Hale.

[36] "Margaret Mead Quotes," BrainyQuote, https://www.brainyquote.com/quotes/margaret_mead_101283.

[37] "Mother Teresa Quotes," BrainyQuote, https://www.brainyquote.com/quotes/mother_teresa_105649.

[38] David Brooks, *The Second Mountain*, (New York: Random House, 2019), 71.

[39] Chambers, *My Utmost for His Highest*, May 18, https://utmost.org/classic/careful-unreasonableness-classic.

Chapter Eight: The Power of Networking

[40] "Dale Carnegie > Quotable Quote," GoodReads, https://www.goodreads.com/quotes/1962-you-can-make-more-friends-in-two-months-by-becoming.

[41] Bob Goff, on Twitter: March 6, 2020; https://twitter.bom>bobgoff>@bobgoff

[42] Martin Buber, *I and Thou* (New York: Charles Scribner's Sons, 1970).

[43] "Mother Teresa Quotes," BrainyQuote, https://www.brainyquote.com/quotes/mother_teresa_107032.

[44] "Phil Callaway Quotes," AZ Quotes, https://www.azquotes.com/author/32597-Phil_Callaway.

[45] David W. Augsburger, *Caring Enough to Hear and Be Heard* (Ada, MI: Baker Pub. Group, 1982), 32.

[46] Bob Goff, *Love Does* (Nashville: Thomas Nelson, 2012), https://goodreads.com/book/show/13497505-love-does

[47] Beverly Chiodo, "Character-Driven Success." https://wwCharacterdrivensuccess.com/services/the-character-driven-success-presentation-2 accessed 5-12-20

[48] "Daniel H. Pink Quotes," BrainyQuote, https://www.brainyquote.com/quotes/daniel_h_pink_521933.

[49] Bernie Siegel, *Prescriptions for Living: Inspirational Lessons for a Joyful, Loving Life* (New York: Random House, 2013), 108.

[50] "George Bernard Shaw Quotes," BrainyQuote, https://www.brainyquote.com/quotes/george_bernard_shaw_122419.

[51] "Elie Wiesel Quotes," BrainyQuote, https://www.brainyquote.com/quotes/elie_wiesel_112798.

[52] "Harry Truman Quotes," BrainyQuote, https://www.brainyquote.com/quotes/harry_s_truman_109615.

[53] Frederick Wm. Faber, *Doubleday Christian Quotation Collection* (New York: Doubleday, 1992), 172.

[54] "Henri Frederic Amiel Quotes," BrainyQuote, https://www.brainyquote.com/quotes/henri_frederic_amiel_148217.

Chapter Nine: Empowering Another's Dream

[55] "Denzel Washington > Quotable Quote," GoodReads, https://www.goodreads.com/quotes/413356-at-the-end-of-the-day-it-s-not-about-what.

[56] Mitt Romney, "Foreign Aid Quotes," BrainyQuote, https://www.brainyquote.com/quotes/mitt_romney_679653?src=t_foreign_aid.

[57] "Robert Kiyosakei Quotes," BrainyQuote, https://www.brainyquote.com/quotes/robert_kiyosaki_385269#:~:text=Robert%20Kiyosaki%20Quotes&text=If%20you%20want%20to%20go%20somewhere%2C%20it%20is%20best%20to,who%20has%20already%20been%20there.

[58] The Lord's Resistance Army is a notorious band of terrorists accused of murder, abduction, and forcing children to participate in hostilities.

[59] "Les Brown Quotes," BrainyQuote, https://www.brainyquote.com/quotes/les_brown_382877.

[60] See the YouTube video called "Sewing Hope" for more details.

[61] "William Halsey Quotes," AZ Quotes, https://www.azquotes.com/author/6149-William_Halsey.

Chapter Ten: The Power of Excellence

[62] "Martin Luther King Jr. > Quotable Quotes," GoodReads, https://www.goodreads.com/quotes/21045-if-a-man-is-called-to-be-a-street-sweeper.

[63] Nahid Bhadelia, "Rage against the Busted Medical Machines," NPR, Sept. 8, 2016, https://www.npr.org/sections/goatsandsoda/2016/09/08/492842274/rage-against-the-busted-medical-machines.

[64] Andrew Jones, "Medical Equipment Donated to Developing Nations Usually Ends Up on the Junk Heap," *Scientific American*, May 6, 2013, https://www.scientificamerican.com/article/medical-equipment-donated-developing-nations-junk-heap.

[65] "Colin Powell Quotes," BrainyQuote, https://www.brainyquote.com/quotes/colin_powell_138130.

[66] "Warren Buffett Quotes," BrainyQuote, https://www.brainyquote.com/quotes/warren_buffett_108887.

[67] Clayton M. Christensen, *How Will You Measure Your Life?* (New York: Harper Collins, 2012), 178.

[68] "Colin Powell Quotes."

[69] Rick Ezell, "Are You a Person of Integrity?" Lifeway.com, Jan. 1, 2014, https://www.lifeway.com/en/articles/parenting-teens-are-you-a-person-of-integrity.

[70] "Martin Luther King Jr. Quotes," BrainyQuote, https://www.brainyquote.com/quotes/martin_luther_king_jr_121315.

[71] Ezell, "Are You a Person of Integrity?"

[72] "Paulo Coelho Quotes," QuoteFancy, https://quotefancy.com/quote/885581/Paulo-Coelho-Don-t-give-up-Normally-it-is-the-last-key-on-the-ring-which-opens-the-door.

[73] "James Michener Quotes," BrainyQuote, https://www.brainyquote.com/quotes/james_a_michener_116031.

[74] "Francis Kelley Quotes," AZ Quotes, https://www.azquotes.com/quote/584761.

[75] "Martin Luther King Jr. Quotes," BrainyQuote.

[76] "Pearl S. Buck Quotes," BrainyQuote, https://www.brainyquote.com/quotes/pearl_s_buck_110942.

Chapter Eleven: Passing on the Passion

[77] "Dillon Burroughs > Quotable Quote," GoodReads, https://www.goodreads.com/quotes/791002-everyone-leaves-a-legacy-whether-they-want-to-or-not.

[78] Chris Marlow, *Doing Good Is Simple: Making a Difference Right Where You Are* (Grand Rapids, MI: Zondervan, 2016), 47

[79] "Tavis Smiley Quotes," QuoteFancy, https://quotefancy.com/quote/1417741/Tavis-Smiley-The-choices-we-make-about-the-lives-we-live-determine-the-kinds-of-legacies.

[80] Dr. R. Kelly Crace, *Authentic Excellence, Giving Voice to Values;* (Routledge; New York, 2020), 127

[81] "Shannon L. Alder > Quotable Quote," GoodReads, https://www.goodreads.com/quotes/455308-carve-your-name-on-hearts-not-tombstones-a-legacy-is.

[82] Christensen, *How Will You Measure Your Life?,* 133–134.

[83] Daniel Scott, "Your Children Are Not Your Legacy," Forbes.com, March 27, 2018, https://www.forbes.com/sites/danielscott1/2018/03/27/your-children-are-not-your-legacy/?sh=76fd83081472.

[84] Christenson, *How Will You Measure Your Life?,* 157.

[85] "Clement Ogedegbe > Quotes," GoodReads, https://www.goodreads.com/author/quotes/17376842.Clement_Ogedegbe.

[86] Jerome C. Glenn, "15 Global Challenges for the Next Decades," OpenMind BBVA, https://www.bbvaopenmind.com/en/articles/15-global-challenges-for-the-next-decades.

[87] Glenn, "15 Global Challenges for the Next Decades."

Chapter Twelve: The Ripple Effect

[88] "Robert F. Kennedy > Quotable Quote," GoodReads, https://www.goodreads.com/quotes/705426-each-time-a-man-stands-up-for-an-ideal-or.

[89] "Laurie Buchanan > Quotable Quote," GoodReads, https://www.goodreads.com/quotes/9291631-our-personal-ripple-effect-is-the-power-of-one-generating.

[90] "Mother Teresa > Quotable Quote," GoodReads, https://www.goodreads.com/quotes/49502-i-alone-cannot-change-the-world-but-i-can-cast.

[91] "Victoria Moran Quotesm" QuoteFancy, https://quotefancy.com/victoria-moran-quotes.

[92] Dennis Merritt Jones, "The Ripple Effect of You," HuffPost, July 25, 2014, https://www.huffpost.com/entry/the-ripple-effect-of-you.

[93] Greg Salciccioli, "The Ripple Effect," Coachwell, https://www.coachwell.com/the-ripple-effect/#.

[94] "C. S. Lewis > Quotable Quote," GoodReads, https://www.goodreads.com/quotes/23353-miracles-are-a-retelling-in-small-letters-of-the-very.

[95] Ellen M. Perry, "Passing on Your Values to the Next Generation," Northwood Family Office, https://www.northwoodfamilyoffice.com/wp-content/uploads/2015/03/Passing-on-Values-to-the-Next-Generation-Ellen-Perry-GenSpring.pdf.